It's Not Just You

Insights from the Canberra Weekly's psychology columnist

Dr Vivienne Lewis

www.ausapress.com
AUSTRALIAN ACADEMIC PRESS

Other books by this author:

Positive Bodies: Loving the Skin You're In

No Body's Perfect: A helper's guide to promoting positive body image in children and young people

Eating Disorders: A Practitioner's Guide to Psychological Care

Embracing You: A Practical Guide to Body Image and Self-Acceptance

Available at www.ausapress.com

First published by
Australian Academic Press Group Pty. Ltd.
www.ausapress.com

NATIONAL LIBRARY OF AUSTRALIA
A catalogue record for this book is available from the National Library of Australia

ISBN 978-1-923114-22-7 (paperback)
ISBN 978-1-923114-23-4 (ebook)

Publisher & Editor: Stephen May
Cover: Australian Academic Press
Typesetting: Australian Academic Press
Printing: Lightning Source

Contents

Acknowledgements

Although my name appears on the cover of this book, *It's Not Just You* is the result of countless conversations, connections, and moments shared with others over many years.

First and foremost, thank you to Canberra Weekly for providing me with a platform to write these columns and for believing that psychology belongs not only in clinics, universities, and textbooks, but also in the everyday lives of ordinary people. It has been a privilege to contribute to a publication that is so deeply connected to the Canberra community.

To the University of Canberra, thank you for supporting my work as both a clinician and academic. For more than two decades, UC has been my professional home, providing opportunities to teach, research, supervise, and engage with the wider community. Many of the ideas explored in these pages have been shaped by the students, colleagues, and experiences I have encountered along the way.

A special thank you to Stephen May at Australian Academic Press for his encouragement and support over many years. Stephen is one of those rare publishers who genuinely cares about people and the positive impact that knowledge can have on their lives. His commitment to making psychological information accessible to the broader community, along with his wisdom, humility, and thoughtful advice, has helped bring not only this book, but all of my books, to life. I am deeply grateful for his belief in my work and for the contribution he continues to make to psychology and education in Australia.

To my students and colleagues, thank you for your curiosity, enthusiasm, challenges, and conversations. Teaching and learning are never one-way processes. Every lecture, supervision session, research meeting, and discussion contributes to the way I think about people and the human experience.

To the readers of my columns, here in Canberra and across Australia and internationally, thank you for welcoming these reflections into your lives. I have been humbled by the emails, messages, and conversations that have followed many of these pieces. Knowing that a column has helped someone feel understood, less alone, or a little more hopeful is one of the greatest privileges of my work. This book exists because of your ongoing support and engagement.

To my friends, thank you for your encouragement, humour, perspective, and unwavering support. Life is richer because of the people we share it with, and I am fortunate to have such wonderful people in mine.

Finally, to my family — particularly my parents, Carmel and Phil — thank you for your love, encouragement, and belief in me. Your support has been a constant throughout every stage of my life and career. You taught me the value of education, curiosity, compassion, and hard work, and those values sit at the heart of everything I do.

As a psychologist, researcher, writer and fellow human being, I am continually reminded that our struggles are often far more universal than we realise. My hope is that somewhere within these pages, readers find understanding, reassurance, a moment of reflection, or simply the comforting reminder that whatever they are facing, they do not have to face it alone.

About the Author

Dr Vivienne Lewis is a clinical psychologist at the University of Canberra specialising in the areas of body image, disordered eating, and eating disorders. Her research focuses on the influence of appearance perceptions on wellbeing and mental health in males and females. Vivienne also has a private practice where she sees clients of all ages dealing with body dissatisfaction, eating disorders, stress, depression and anxiety. She is part of the University of Canberra experts guide and regularly features in the media. Vivienne is a member of the professional body, the Australian Psychological Society College of Clinical Psychologists. She is a Board Approved Supervisor and supervises clinical students, registrars and fully qualified psychologists. She also offers workshops and supervision to a range of professionals working with people with disordered eating and body image issues and is a strong advocate for body respect and celebrating body diversity. This is Vivienne's fifth book. Vivienne's University of Canberra research profile can be found online at:

https://researchprofiles.canberra.edu.au/en/persons/vivienne-lewis

Introduction

For many years, my professional life has been devoted to understanding what drives people's behaviour, how they think, feel, and come to see themselves in the world. As a clinical psychologist, an academic at the University of Canberra, and author working in the areas of body image, eating disorders and self-worth, I spend my days listening to stories — stories of struggle, resilience, self-criticism, courage and growth. Again and again, I am reminded that beneath our individual circumstances, we share common fears, doubts and hopes.

When psychologists talk about mental health, we are not simply talking about mental illness. Mental health is something we all have. It refers to our psychological, emotional and social wellbeing — the way we think, feel, behave, cope with stress, relate to others and navigate the ups and downs of everyday life. Just as our physical health can vary from day to day, so too can our mental health. Feeling anxious before a big presentation, grieving the loss of someone you love, feeling overwhelmed by work, or doubting yourself from time to time are all part of being human. Good mental health does not mean being happy all the time. Rather, it is about understanding ourselves, responding to life's challenges as best we can, and finding ways to care for ourselves and others along the way.

Outside the therapy room and lecture theatre, I have long believed that psychological knowledge should not be reserved for textbooks or clinical settings. It should be accessible, practical and human — something people can recognise themselves in, perhaps while reading over a morning coffee.

That belief is what led me, somewhat unexpectedly, to writing for the *Canberra Weekly*.

The column began with a simple invitation: could I write short, practical pieces translating psychological research into everyday language? The answer, it turned out, was yes — and also no. Yes, I could share the science and my research. But what readers responded to most were the stories, the moments of recognition, the permission to be imperfect, and the gentle humour that reminds us we are all gloriously human.

Week by week, the column became a conversation with the community. Readers wrote to say they felt less alone in their struggles with self-doubt, parenting pressures, grief, ageing, relationships, body image, or simply the exhaustion of trying to hold life together. Some shared that they clipped columns to keep beside their beds. Others passed them to friends. Many said, 'I thought it was just me.'

This book gathers those reflections together.

Within these pages you will find themes that echo through everyday life: self-care that goes beyond bubble baths, the quiet work of building self-worth, navigating anxiety and change, living in bodies we don't always feel at peace with, coping with loss, finding meaning in work and relationships, and learning to treat ourselves with the same compassion we offer others.

While grounded in psychology, these pieces were written for real life — for busy mornings, difficult evenings, and the ordinary moments in between when we are trying our best.

There is no right way to read this book. You may choose to start at the beginning and work your way through, or you may dip in and out, turning to the parts and topics that resonate most with you at a particular moment in your life. Each column was originally written as a standalone reflection, so they can be read in any order. Some may offer practical strategies, others may provide a different perspective, and some may simply remind you that what you are experiencing is a shared part of the human condition. My suggestion is to read slowly, pause when something resonates, and perhaps return to particular pieces when life presents new challenges. Often, the lessons we need most reveal themselves at exactly the right time.

If you are reading this book, you may be navigating a challenging season, supporting someone you love, or simply curious about how to live with a little more ease and self-acceptance. Wherever you find yourself, my hope is that these pages offer reassurance, insight and companionship.

You will not find perfection here.

You will find permission.

Permission to be human. Permission to be unfinished. Permission to care for yourself in ways that are steady rather than dramatic. Permission to recognise your worth.

If something in these pages helps you feel seen, understood, or just a little kinder toward yourself, then this book has done its work.

And if, as you read, you occasionally nod, laugh, or think 'that's me,' then please know: you are not alone.

Part 1

Understanding Yourself and Your Emotions

Having a bad day?

I've seen first hand how small shifts in mindset can significantly improve mental health, especially when it comes to the start and end of the day. Difficult days happen to everyone, including me, and they can be triggered by stress, unmet expectations, or just the unpredictability of life. However, there are practical steps we can take to help turn a tough day around.

First, it's important to remember that a bad day doesn't mean your life is bad. Everyone experiences conflict, stress, or mistakes — it's part of being human. When things go wrong, it doesn't mean you're a bad person. What matters most is how we respond. Whether through apologising, making amends, or reflecting on what we've learned, it's essential not to hold onto guilt or label ourselves negatively. A challenging moment is just that — a moment.

Resisting the urge to generalise is equally important. It's easy to think that one bad day means everything is falling apart. However, seeing a tough day as temporary — just one chapter in a much larger story — helps prevent negative thinking patterns like 'nothing ever goes right for me'. This shift in perspective can make it easier to move forward.

When setting yourself up for a better day, starting with intention can help. The way you begin your morning often determines how the rest of the day unfolds. Instead of diving straight into emails or social media, take a few moments to breathe, stretch, or reflect on something positive. Personally, I like to spend time with my coffee, thinking about three things I'm grateful for. Gratitude helps shift the focus from what's wrong to what's going well, even on tough days.

Movement is another powerful tool for improving mood. You don't need to do a long workout — a simple walk outside can help clear your mind and reduce tension. Taking a brief break, even from a stressful situation, allows you to reset and refocus. Spending time in nature, noticing the trees or birds, helps ground us and brings a sense of calm.

Regular eating and a good night's sleep are crucial for mental wellbeing. As a clinical psychologist, I often see how skipping meals or poor sleep can heighten stress and negatively affect mood. Eating balanced meals throughout the day helps maintain energy levels and stabilises mood, while proper rest allows your body and mind to recharge, enabling you to face the next day with more resilience.

Human connection is also vital for improving mental health. Reaching out to someone, whether it's a friend, family member, or trusted person, reminds us that we are not alone. Even small interactions — a supportive text or a kind word — can shift our perspective.

Remember to breathe. Pausing for a few deep breaths can help centre you during stressful moments.

On the hardest days, prioritise doing at least one thing that brings you joy, such as listening to music, reading, or spending time with a friend. These small acts of self-care aren't indulgences; they're essential for maintaining wellbeing. Finding what works for you is key, and these moments are investments in your health.

Above all, practise kindness to yourself. Ask, 'Would I say this to a friend?' When you catch yourself being critical, shift toward compassion. Reflecting on three things that went well in the day, even if it's as simple as you got through a tough day, helps you have a more positive mindset.

If you're noticing more bad days than good for more than a few weeks it's a great idea to reach out to someone for help such as a psychologist or counsellor.

Coping with boredom

Feeling bored is a common emotion that arises when we are not interested or engaged in an activity. It's seen as a negative experience and most of us have felt it. An example is when you are in a work meeting or in class and are not interested in listening and are getting frustrated and restless with the content or delivery.

Although boredom is normal, for some, this feeling can have negative consequences. For instance, it can make it hard to concentrate when we need to pay attention, stop us learning and make us feel angry. This, in turn, can affect our interactions with others and our behaviour such as expressing our boredom in a way that gets us into trouble. Think for example, where a child may get told off for not paying attention or where we might express anger and irritability verbally.

Another problem with boredom is that people feel unmotivated and become unproductive. We can then engage in meaningless and mindless activities. Boredom can, for some people, increase their likelihood of being disruptive. When we feel bored, we crave stimulation, and some people may seek it in ways that lead to trouble, such as engaging in risky behaviours like substance use or making impulsive decisions in an attempt to find something novel and exciting.

It's not possible to always be entertained and never be bored but it's important that we have ways to cope with it when it happens and also minimise its occurrence. Here are some strategies:

Do mentally stimulating activities at work and play. Finding what we are interested in and passionate about is important to make our lives meaningful and interesting. It might be a hobby, a type of work, a research interest or a sport.

Do activities that you enjoy and are mentally stimulating regularly. Find things you find pleasure in and can access for different amounts of time. For example, what can you do if you only have a few minutes if you don't have hours to do something?

Know what your strengths and weaknesses are. If you're not good at sitting still for long periods, have regular breaks and move your body regularly. Try not to expect others to do this either, such as children.

Set time limits for activities with rewards for completion. This helps motivate us to continue with tasks we don't enjoy such as household chores.

Do regular, mentally stimulating things but also allow downtime. We have to teach our brains to cope with relaxation and lack of stimulation so our brains can revitalise and replenish. Resting is actually productive.

Moving our body regularly can also help with boredom as it releases endorphins that lift our mood and release the frustration we can feel when we are bored.

Socially engage with people whose company you enjoy. Have fun with your friends or engage in an interesting debate.

As adults, we often have to help children explore and find new ways to express themselves, so they don't get bored also.

How to unwind

How many of us are feeling stressed right now? Like you can't relax or unwind, you've got too much on? Do you catch yourself saying 'I don't have time to relax'? If you are saying this, then making a conscious decision to give yourself time for relaxation and rest is what's needed. There will never be a right time, we have to decide to work on it right now or it will never happen. Learning to relax is like any skill, we have to make a decision it's worth doing and then practice doing it.

Why is relaxation important?

Calming ourselves and focusing on something enjoyable or peaceful helps both our brain and body. When our body is relaxed it's relieved of pain and tension and keeps our heart and immune system healthy. When we are more relaxed our mind is clearer, our memory is better, we feel less anxious and stressed, our mood improves and we and those around us benefit. So how do you relax?

Prioritise yourself

Why is it that we can prioritise everyone else but not ourselves? We need to learn to say, 'I am worthwhile' and value ourselves. We deserve care and rest just like anyone else. You know the metaphor, 'put your oxygen mask on first before helping others'? Well, we are no good to others if we are not okay ourselves. For those who have children, think about role-modelling self-care behaviours such as showing ourselves relaxing and stating that we are doing something for downtime.

It helps to set times during the day for relaxation; like making the time to go for a walk, have a cup of tea, stop for a minute, play some music whilst doing tasks you don't like, reading a book. Making frequent, short periods during the day our relaxation and self-care ensures it happens. Try not to multitask a few times throughout the day and just do one thing at a time; sit down and eat lunch undisturbed, take your tea breaks at work, finish work on time and allow others to help. Sometimes we need to stop and reset.

Work out what relaxes you

Write a list of all the things that help you relax — from something that takes a few seconds to things that take a few hours or a whole day. Stepping outside to breathe in some fresh air can also re-set the brain particularly when it's stuffy inside. Does watching your favourite show relax you or sitting in the sun during lunch, chatting with friends? Fresh air, sleep, food, and exercise are key. Work out what your thing is and do it. You are important.

If you're really struggling, talking to someone like a psychologist about your worries and troubles, can be helpful.

Coping with feelings of anger

Feeling angry is a normal emotion. However, it is how we express that anger and what we do with this feeling that's important.

What is anger?

Anger can range from a feeling of momentary annoyance to full-on rage where we lose control, and we might yell or lash out. We can tell when we are angry because our heart rate and blood pressure rise and our adrenaline kicks in which can be unhealthy for our body if it's ongoing and unresolved. Not to mention, it also has an emotional impact on others.

Why do we feel anger?

Anger is actually an instinct to feeling threatened, think of an animal fighting with another animal because they are defending their offspring. As humans though, this aggressive type of response to a threat can occur at times when it's not helpful, such as in the workplace or with our loved ones. Yelling and screaming in most situations is not socially acceptable and certainly, there is no excuse for using physical violence.

What healthy things can we do then when we feel angry?

The best way is to **be assertive** and **express your needs** and feelings without hurting others through your words or actions. Sometimes people misinterpret being assertive as being pushy or demanding or yelling out your feelings. But assertiveness actually refers to being clear about your needs in a respectful and calm way to others.

Often people are reluctant to talk about their feelings and their needs, leading to resentment. This can cause internal anger and passive-aggressive behaviour, characterised by not openly expressing our feelings or needs. Instead, we might hold grudges, plan revenge, speak negatively about others behind their backs, or belittle them. Such behavior fosters bitterness and unhappiness.

If you recognise your anger as unjust and irrational, perhaps because you're in a bad mood or your perception is skewed, it's important to find a way to calm down. Remove yourself from the situation, do some deep breathing or relaxation, talk to someone helpful to get things off your chest and think of a constructive way to address the issue that's making you angry. We also need to learn to let some things go, holding a grudge only makes us feel bad and it doesn't solve the issue.

Work out **what triggers your anger** and learn ways to deal with it in a **calm** manner. Question if you're thinking rationally or if it is because you have a low tolerance due to physical illness or pain. Are you lacking sleep or hungry? Whatever the reason, addressing it will help you have more healthy interactions with others.

Are you over-angry?

If you feel that your or someone else's anger is out of control, frightening, or happening frequently, talk to someone who can help.

Sensing a sense of achievement

Feeling a sense of achievement is a very important part of feeling positive about ourselves. It's when we feel proud of ourselves for having achieved something difficult or worthwhile to us. And it's all relative, it doesn't matter if others might have found the task easy, if we struggle with something and achieve it, then we deserve to feel good about it. Achievements come in many shapes and forms such as doing a task you really don't want to do such as cleaning the house or completing a work or study task that is mentally challenging.

Validate yourself

Sometimes people look for external validation, like praise, for their accomplishments. We need to learn to praise ourselves as this is much better for our self-esteem. It doesn't have to be visible to others and a lot of our achievements aren't. At the same time, it's important, especially for children, to be praised and validated for hard things they may do, such as coping with something stressful, finishing a chore, helping a friend or being kind when they could have easily not been.

Write down your achievements

Every day we achieve things and it's important to acknowledge it. Sometimes writing down the challenging things you've done in a day or week helps us to see what we've done. It might be as simple as getting through a meeting at work you were worried about, speaking up in class when you usually don't, or getting something in the house or car fixed.

Break tasks down

If you're feeling a lack of achievement over something difficult, try to break the task down into smaller steps and celebrate completing these. For example, if a child is struggling to understand maths, break the learning up into achievable, manageable chunks for them, be encouraging and supportive, and celebrate their success. We know that all of us learn better when we feel we can achieve things that are meaningful to us, and it leads to better health and wellbeing. It gives us confidence in ourselves that if we make our goals realistic, we can do hard things.

Celebrate the steps

Celebrate all the steps. This is particularly important for students. Rather than waiting to celebrate at the end of the school year or graduation, celebrate completing each assignment or test and progressing with your learning daily. What reading did you get done today or what new information have you acquired?

Mental health achievements

Focus also on achievements that are social and part of our wellbeing such as relaxation goals and better sleep. Looking after our body by moving it every day and eating well are big achievements in our busy lives.

Feeling good about ourselves and our lives means we are doing things that propel us forward as well as coping with challenges and adversity. It's not about doing it perfectly but doing what is in our mental health best interests.

Fostering a positive self-worth

Self-worth is important to our mental health and wellbeing and refers to seeing oneself as valuable and important as a human being. It encompasses the understanding that each person is valuable and deserving of respect, regardless of external achievements, appearances, or opinions of others. It is not about feeling better than others but rather being able to respect yourself and treat yourself with kindness no matter what is happening in your life, especially during times of struggle. Here are ten key strategies to enhance self-worth:

1. **Assess where your beliefs about self-worth come from.** Understanding the origins of your negative beliefs is crucial. These beliefs often stem from family, peers, or media. Reflect on your experiences — if you grew up hearing critical comments or were influenced by societal expectations, consider how these messages shaped your views. Reframing these beliefs can promote a healthier sense of self.
2. **Challenge negative thoughts**. Identify negative thoughts about yourself, such as 'I'm not good enough' or 'I'll never succeed'. Ask yourself, *Is this really true?* Challenging these thoughts helps you

adopt a more balanced perspective, such as 'My value isn't determined by my achievements'.

3. **Appreciate your strengths.** Shift your focus from perceived flaws to your strengths and accomplishments. Whether it's being a good friend, a dedicated worker, or someone who cares for others, appreciating your unique qualities fosters gratitude. This perspective reinforces the idea that your worth isn't solely tied to external validation.
4. **Challenge unrealistic expectations.** Societal standards often promote unattainable ideals. When you catch yourself thinking, 'I should be more successful' or 'I should have a perfect life', question those standards. Reframe your thoughts to acknowledge that everyone's journey is unique and valuable.
5. **Practice self-compassion.** Many individuals are hard on themselves, especially regarding perceived failures. Practising self-compassion means treating yourself with kindness. Engage in positive self-talk, write affirmations, or participate in activities that bring you joy. These acts cultivate a more supportive inner dialogue.
6. **Limit social comparison.** Social comparison can lead to feelings of inadequacy. If you find yourself comparing your life to others, remind yourself that everyone is on their own path and has unique strengths. This mindset helps reduce the pressure to conform to external standards.
7. **Cultivate gratitude for your accomplishments.** Gratitude is a powerful tool for fostering positive self-worth. Keeping a gratitude journal where you note what you appreciate about yourself — like overcom-

ing challenges or helping others — shifts your focus from perceived shortcomings to strengths, helping you develop a healthier sense of self.

8. **Engage in fulfilling activities.** Participate in activities that bring you joy, whether it's volunteering, pursuing hobbies, or spending time with loved ones. Focusing on what makes you happy allows you to reconnect with your sense of purpose and self-worth.
9. **Use exposure to challenge insecurities.** Gradually expose yourself to situations that trigger feelings of inadequacy. Start with small steps, like sharing ideas in a group or taking on new responsibilities. This exposure can help reduce anxiety and build confidence over time.
10. **Surround yourself with supportive people.** Your social circle significantly influences how you view yourself. Surround yourself with people who uplift and support you. Positive relationships can reinforce your sense of self-worth and help you see your value.

By applying these strategies, you can shift away from negative beliefs and develop a healthier, more positive sense of self-worth. Embracing self-acceptance is a lifelong journey that can lead to greater overall well-being.

How to start your day on the right foot

Do you wake up in the morning full of energy and looking forward to the day? (I hear you laughing). Well maybe on days off or when something exciting is happening like a holiday or seeing your favourite band. On a serious note, many people wake up feeling tired, unmotivated to get out of bed, dreading the day ahead, or stressed because there's so much to do. So, how do we wake up feeling the best we can and start our day as calm and content as possible? Here are a few tips.

Don't rush getting up

Many of us get up in a rush and so we start our day already feeling stressed. Try setting the alarm just a little bit earlier so you can ease yourself out of bed or have a bit of me time before you get the kids ready for the day or get to work.

Do something enjoyable first up

Do you need to move your routine around, so you have something to look forward to when you first wake up? You could make your favourite breakfast, do a social sport, read your book, watch a bit of TV or enjoy a coffee.

Be prepared the night before

Get ready the night before so you're not rushing in the morning. Lay your clothes out for the day ahead, get your lunch and snacks ready to grab on your way out, put your medications out and have all you need ready to go.

Get a good night's sleep

Getting a good night's sleep is also important. Plan to go to bed at a reasonable time, do your relaxation well before you're tired, get ready for bed earlier and make sure your bed and room are comfortable for sleeping. Simple tips include ensuring you're not too hot or cold, your room is dark and quiet enough, you feel relaxed before getting into bed and turn off your devices in plenty of time, so they don't keep you awake.

Have some calm on the way to work and school

On your way to work or school, leave plenty of time so you're not rushing through traffic. Put something relaxing on to listen to in the car or do some deep breathing and talk to yourself calmly.

Take it one step at a time

It's quite normal for individuals to experience mood fluctuations during the day, and mornings can be particularly tough for some. Keep it simple and take it one step at a time. When you first wake up, don't think about the whole day ahead, just think about getting a cup of tea or having some breakfast. Your mood often improves as the day goes on.

Talk to someone

If you're really struggling with low mood, anxiety and stress every morning, you might find talking to someone, like a psychologist, about your worries and troubles helpful.

Mental health goal setting for a new year

The start of a new year is an excellent time to reflect on your mental wellbeing and plan for positive changes. Consider what habits or experiences from the past year energised you and what drained your energy. For example, did regular exercise, spending time outdoors, or connecting with loved ones help you feel more balanced? On the other hand, did overcommitting, skipping rest, or excessive screen time leave you feeling depleted? Reflecting on these patterns can guide you in making thoughtful adjustments.

Set realistic goals that are clear and achievable. Instead of broadly aiming to 'sleep better,' try a specific goal like, 'I'll go to bed by 10:30pm on weeknights.' Goals aligned with your personal values — such as improving your health, deepening relationships, or creating more downtime — are often more fulfilling and motivating.

Planning self-care activities and scheduling them into your routine is key to maintaining your wellbeing. Small, consistent actions like setting aside 15 minutes daily to read, meditate, or enjoy a hobby can have a big impact over time. Regular physical activity — whether it's walking, dancing, or yoga — can also boost your mood and energy levels. The key is to choose activities that bring you joy and fit into your lifestyle.

It's also important to anticipate challenges that might interfere with self-care and create backup plans. If bad weather makes outdoor exercise difficult, prepare an indoor alternative like a workout video. If stress gets in the way, try quick relaxation techniques like deep breathing or grounding exercises to help you refocus. Thinking ahead makes it easier to stay consistent with your goals, even when obstacles arise.

Learning to say no to commitments that drain your energy is another valuable habit. Protecting your time allows you to focus on what truly matters. For example, instead of automatically agreeing to every request, try saying, 'I'd love to help, but I'm not able to right now.' Similarly, reducing time spent on social media can free up space for more meaningful activities. You might set limits, such as no social media an hour before bed or taking one 'screen-free' day each week.

Regularly reviewing your goals and adjusting them as needed helps you stay on track. If exercising every day feels overwhelming, scale back to three times a week and incorporate gentler activities on other days. Flexibility ensures that your goals remain achievable and sustainable.

Taking time to care for yourself is not only essential for your wellbeing but also helps you show up fully for others. By reflecting on what works, setting clear goals, and planning for obstacles, you can create a year filled with balance, energy, and joy.

The importance of taking breaks

When work, uni or school gets busy and holidays seem far away, it's actually a great time to get into some good mental health work/study habits. My clients and students regularly come to me saying they are exhausted and just trying to get to the end of a hard slog before they can stop. But if the break is still a few months away, then just continuing on and busting your gut to get to the end is not the best way to go.

Regarding exams, the strategy often taken, especially by students, is to study for long periods, often feeling guilty when one takes time out. Our brains can usually only concentrate for about 40 minutes at maximum capacity and after this point, our level of absorption of material or ability to think straight diminishes. Rather than trying to just push through when we are tired or struggling to concentrate, we are better off taking a mindful break for a few minutes.

When we are at work, people's ability to concentrate fully on a task is dependent on the task at hand, how engaged we are with the task, whether we are hydrated and have eaten recently and how rested we are. For an average eight-hour workday, we need a good 20–30 minute-break about every two hours in order to reset and refresh.

What do we mean by taking a break?

A break is when we disengage from an intense activity (such as study) and actively rest our thinking brain. A break can be a few seconds just to stretch our physical body or a few minutes to focus on some basic needs and self-care, such as having something to eat, a drink of water, a short walk or doing some deep breathing. It's something that fuels our body and brain. It's important to have regular breaks otherwise our bodies become stiff and sore, our brains overworked, and we feel lethargic or stressed.

What should we avoid doing when taking a break?

Because the aim of a break is to give our brain rest and fuel our body, mindless activities such as scrolling on our phones or engaging with social media are best avoided. Our brain doesn't recover from mindless activities. Rather, we should engage in mindful activities, activities where we gain energy and refreshment, such as food, water and relaxed movement.

Getting enough sleep is important, as well as having time off from study. We can't constantly study as there comes a point where our brain cannot absorb anymore, and we just start to feel tired and irritable.

On the flip side, if you're struggling from procrastination, try timetabling short periods of study or work with the reward of a pleasant activity afterwards.

Remember that it's okay to take breaks and have days off even when we are working towards a deadline such as exams. Breaks help keep us alert and refreshed and make us more resilient during times of stress.

Why can't I say no?

It's one of the first words we learn as infants. In fact, as parents, we actively encourage our infants and children to be able to say 'No'. 'Do you want this to eat? — No'. 'Do you want to play with this? — No'. 'Do you want to do this? — No'.

So, why is it so hard as adults to say no? My clients constantly tell me that they are feeling overwhelmed and over committed because they can't say no. Common things such as agreeing to do things we don't want to do, to see people we don't want to spend time with, to go to events we don't want to attend. It can be frustrating, stressful, and anxiety-inducing. My clients commonly say, 'I want to say no but I feel that I can't'.

Why do we do this? It can be for several reasons. One is that we don't like to deal with negative emotions like people being upset with us or disappointed. Another can be the need to be liked and approved of. Sometimes it's because we like to feel needed. Other times it can be that we don't want to make someone angry. Or maybe we feel we 'should' say yes.

What's the consequence of not saying no?

By not saying no when we don't want to do something or overcommitting to things, we neglect our own needs and cause ourselves extra stress. We can also worry about saying no and the consequences.

However, if you always say 'yes' to everyone, people will continue to ask and expect you to agree. We are saying, 'I will always put other's needs first at the expense of my own needs.' This makes us unhappy in the long-term. We may resent others, and feel they are taking advantage of us.

When we constantly try to please others, we are not listening to our own needs. Saying no does not make us selfish — this is a common worry — rather, it helps us preserve our resources for things that are really important to say yes to.

How do we learn to say no? Well, we have to practise!

Practise saying no to easier things. For example, saying no to options a person might give, such as a food or outings choice.

Start telling people what you do want and make your needs clearer. Your needs are just as valid as anyone else's. Remember the metaphor of putting your own oxygen mask on first before you can help others.

Remind yourself that you can't please everyone and not everyone will like you. As uncomfortable as this thought is, we have to stop people pleasing at the expense of our own needs. This is not selfish, it's about self-preservation!

Lastly, if you feel caught off guard with a request, tell the person you'll get back to them or you'll have to think about it. That gives you time to work out your 'no' response.

Leave your phone alone!

How many of us panic when we realise we have forgotten our phone or haven't checked it in a while (like seconds) for a message? How often is that message or feed about anything important or useful?

Mobile phone addiction is a real phenomenon, particularly in youth, where one simply cannot go without their phone. That fear of missing out or 'needing' it for entertainment is real. Research has shown that heavy smartphone and social media use increases mental health issues, including anxiety and depression, especially in young people. Frequent use has been linked to decreased attention and concentration (being totally focused on your phone) as well as sleep deprivation (all that nighttime 'talking' and scrolling). Also, comparisons to others through social media can lead to body image and self-esteem issues due to feeling less than others. That fear of missing out when you see friends having fun without you or feeling that others are more perfect (thanks to filtering) or have better lives (rarely do people show themselves having a bad day).

I see a lot of parents and young people in my work and the battle over phone use is a standard problem.

How do I get my child to stop using their phone, is a constant question.

What do we do?

Ok adults, we have to role model the behaviour we want our kids to follow — turn your phone off and start engaging in real-life interactions at home. Find alternatives, what can you do instead of using your phone?

Maybe don't go cold turkey but gradually cut down the use and reinforce non-phone use with rewards and fun activities. Notice the benefits of not being on your phone, such as better sleep, less anxiety, less worry about misinterpreting messages, more play and emotional conversations.

Have **phone-free time** at home and establish some family rules around everyone (yes, everyone) putting their phone away and turning them off at a certain time at night, for the whole night.

Young people often worry: 'What if my friend needs me?' Trust me, no good messages come overnight. Try sending a message to your friends about when they can and can't contact you, that way they know to get you before your phone goes off. Experiment with turning your phone off and see how much better you sleep.

Go old-fashioned. If you use your phone for music or as an alarm, get an alarm clock or music player.

Talk to your child about the times they feel negative when using their phone. Think about how you feel when you socially compare yourself to others or have negative interactions with your peers. What is a break from that like?

Remember you're teaching your kids life skills including getting good sleep, being able to entertain oneself without devices and being able to have real-life, in-person conversations. It's hard work and it doesn't always work the first time but keep calm and don't give up.

Part 2

Body Image, Food, and Self-Acceptance

Weight loss goals and the impact on mental health

As a specialist in body image concerns and eating disorders, I want to share insights into the relationship between weight loss and mental health. While the desire to lose weight is common, it's crucial to understand that weight loss can have significant emotional and psychological consequences, especially for those with body image issues or eating disorders.

Many of my clients come to me believing that losing weight will solve their self-esteem issues. They think that if they can reach a certain weight, they will feel happier, more confident and more accepted. However, even after weight loss, many still struggle with low self-esteem and negative body image. Self-worth cannot be based solely on appearance or the number on the scale.

A major concern arises when people are told by healthcare professionals, family or friends that they need to lose weight for their health. While health is important, this message can have unintended psychological effects. The pressure to lose weight often leads to shame, guilt and anxiety about one's body. For individuals with a history of eating disorders or body image struggles, the focus on weight can intensify unhealthy behaviours like restrictive eating or excessive exercise.

Weight loss is often driven by the desire to look better according to societal standards. The media often glorify specific body types, which can distort our perception of beauty. Many individuals pursue weight loss in hopes of feeling more attractive or desirable, but this can lead to a never-ending cycle of comparison. Even when weight loss is achieved, dissatisfaction may persist because the idealised beauty standard is unrealistic and unachievable. This constant comparison can create a deeper sense of inadequacy.

It's essential to shift focus from weight loss to prioritising overall health and wellbeing. Health goes beyond the number on the scale—it involves physical, mental and emotional balance. Focusing solely on weight loss can overshadow a more holistic approach, which includes nourishing your body, staying active, getting enough sleep and fostering positive mental health. By focusing on health, rather than weight, we can cultivate sustainable habits that promote well-being, regardless of whether weight loss occurs.

The obsession with weight loss can also contribute to disordered eating behaviours, such as restrictive dieting or binge eating. When the pursuit of weight loss becomes all-consuming, it leads to deprivation and unhealthy relationships with food. This cycle can trigger binge eating, guilt and further restriction, potentially evolving into eating disorders such as bulimia nervosa or binge eating disorder.

If you're considering weight loss, it's important to be mindful of its impact on your mental health. Focus on building a healthy relationship with food, practising self-compassion and prioritising emotional wellbeing. Your worth isn't determined by the scale, and true wellbeing comes from caring for both your body and mind. A healthy approach to weight loss should always prioritise emotional health alongside physical goals.

How dopamine affects eating and pleasure

I work with many people who struggle with their relationship with food. Eating isn't just about hunger — it's also tied to emotions and pleasure. We often eat when we're bored, stressed, upset or anxious because food can provide comfort. This happens because of dopamine, a brain chemical linked to pleasure and reward.

Turning to food for comfort isn't necessarily bad, unless it becomes our only way to cope, leads to guilt and shame or affects our health. Understanding dopamine can help us find other ways to improve our mood without relying on food.

Why food feels rewarding

Dopamine is known as the 'feel-good' chemical because it motivates us and reinforces behaviours that bring pleasure. When we eat foods high in sugar, fat or salt, our brain releases dopamine, making us feel good. Over time, our brain starts linking food with emotional relief, which can lead to emotional eating and overeating. However, this dopamine boost is short-lived. Once the pleasure fades, we may feel guilty or still stressed, creating a cycle of emotional eating. Plus, frequent dopamine spikes from food can make us crave more, leading to eating habits that may not be the best for us.

Other ways to boost dopamine

To break the cycle of emotional eating, it helps to find other sources of pleasure and reward. Here are some effective, research-backed, strategies I share with my clients:

- **Exercise:** Physical activity naturally increases dopamine and releases endorphins, improving mood and reducing stress.
- **Listen to music:** Enjoying music, especially songs with positive memories, can trigger dopamine release and improve mood.
- **Connect with others:** Spending time with friends, family or pets can boost dopamine and provide emotional support.
- **Engage in hobbies:** Creative activities like drawing, painting, writing or playing an instrument give a sense of achievement and satisfaction.
- **Practice mindfulness and relaxation:** Deep breathing, meditation and progressive muscle relaxation help regulate emotions and promote well-being.
- **Acts of kindness:** Helping others, whether through volunteering, giving compliments or small gestures, creates a natural dopamine boost.
- **Set and achieve small goals:** Completing small tasks, like cleaning up, finishing a book or learning something new, activates the brain's reward system.

I encourage my clients to write a list of 100 alternative activities to eating, varying in time and effort. This helps them develop healthier coping strategies instead of always turning to food. Food should be enjoyed, but it shouldn't be our only tool for managing emotions. By finding different ways to boost dopamine, we can create a balanced approach to self-care, leading to better mental and physical well-being.

Working with people with eating disorders

I've worked with many people struggling with eating disorders, severe mental health conditions that deeply affect a person's relationship with food and their body. They often involve extreme behaviours that take a serious toll on both physical and mental health. When you see people recover and regain control over their lives with the right support, therapy and care, it's wonderful. It's inspiring to witness the positive changes people make when they start addressing the underlying emotional struggles and unhealthy behaviours. There are a few myths about eating disorders that can make it harder for people to get help and I want to clear some of these up.

Eating disorders are just about food. Eating disorders often serve as a way of coping with deeper emotional issues, like stress, anxiety, or past trauma. For example, one of my clients found that she would restrict her eating when she felt overwhelmed with her workload or her family situation. Food became a way for her to feel in control during chaotic times.

Only women get eating disorders. Around 1 in 4 people with eating disorders are male, but they often don't get the help they need because of stereotypes about men and body image. I treat many males, some aged in their 60s and 70s.

Eating disorders are a choice. Eating disorders are not a choice or something someone does for attention. They are serious mental health conditions that develop from a mix of factors, including biology, life experiences, and mental health struggles. For instance, many of my clients' eating disorders develop after years of dealing with bullying and feeling pressured to meet society's unrealistic beauty standards.

You have to be underweight to have an eating disorder. Eating disorders don't always mean someone is underweight and you can't tell from looking at someone if they have an eating disorder. Eating disorders affect people of all sizes and the focus of treatment is on behaviours and mental health.

People with eating disorders just want attention. Most people with eating disorders feel ashamed and hide their behaviours.

Eating disorders can affect anyone, regardless of age, gender, or background. Binge-eating disorder, the most common, is especially important to recognise, as it affects many people who don't fit the stereotypical image of someone with an eating disorder.

If you or someone you know is struggling with an eating disorder, it's important to seek help early. Eating disorders can cause serious health problems, but with the right treatment, such as therapy, medical and nutritional support, recovery is possible.

Eating disorders in middle age

When thinking of the stereotype of someone with an eating disorder, most people will describe an adolescent female who is underweight. We don't think about women or men in their 40s and 50s with eating disorders, but this is a common period of life where a person can continue to suffer from an eating disorder they've had for many years or develop one for the first time.

An eating disorder is a severe mental health condition where a person is significantly distressed by and preoccupied with their size, shape and weight. This influences their eating (under or overeating), exercise behaviour (such as spending hours exercising to compensate for eating), as well as their happiness, anxiety and ability to socialise (not wanting to eat in front of others is common). Some even turn to the use of weight loss medications, which can be dangerous, or abuse of laxatives or diet pills or deliberately vomiting after eating.

The reason why it is common in middle age is due to all the changes occurring at this time. For women, it may be triggered by changes in hormones and metabolism associated with menopause or pre-menopause. For both men and women, it can be due to a perception that they are moving further and further away from 'idealised' images of youth and thinness portrayed in the media, or muscularity for men. Clients I see in my practice often talk about feeling invisible, no longer getting positive attention for their appearance or getting unwanted attention due to their size and feeling unattractive. It's often harder in middle age to keep fit and healthy due to work and family commitments and so weight gain is common which can lead some to feel very dissatisfied with their bodies and preoccupied with losing weight. Binge eating, feeling a loss of control over one's eating and eating for emotional reasons can become more common in middle age as stress builds up.

So, what can adults in middle and older age do to help themselves? It's about recognising there may be a problem and being brave and getting help, talking to your doctor or a psychologist about your worries. As well as working on your perception of yourself and your body, celebrate your body for what it can do, not what it looks like. Focus on your qualities and strengths — what your friends and family love about you. Get away from social media that promotes diet culture and unrealistic images of what men and women are supposed to look like. Embrace your uniqueness, do nice things for your body, make it feel good and talk to it in respectful ways.

Self-compassion and body image

A positive body image is when we appreciate and are respectful towards our bodies regardless of their appearance. I see many clients of all ages and gender identities that really struggle with negative body image, not liking their bodies and seeing flaws in them. We live in a world where we are bombarded by unhelpful messages about unrealistic beauty standards and there are many myths and negative stereotypes attributed to certain body types. Unfortunately, it's been normalised to feel dissatisfied with our appearance. Often the things we say to our bodies (and selves) are the things we would never say to a friend. We can be cruel and mean to ourselves such as saying, 'I'm stupid', 'I'm a failure', or 'I'm unlovable', making us feel bad and demotivated.

I talk to my clients about the concept of self-compassion, which involves being kind to ourselves (just like we would to a friend), realising and acknowledging when we are struggling and hurting, and comforting ourselves. For example, on a bad day, try saying to yourself, 'Today is hard, and I acknowledge that I'm not feeling great. What can I do to make this day better?' Then, think about how you can seek comfort or soothe yourself. Applying this to body image might mean recognising that you're not feeling great about your body but choosing to replace harsh words with kind ones and doing something that makes your body feel better. This approach can completely transform how you relate to your body and feel about it. Practising self-compassion can improve all aspects of our lives by helping relieve suffering, making us feel less alone, and increasing awareness of our needs. Some ways to do this include:

- **Be aware of your thoughts about yourself.** Observe your thoughts and feelings and notice negative self-talk without becoming overwhelmed by it. Acknowledge that it might be there, but it doesn't make it true and you don't have to do anything to harm or punish yourself as a result. You might also think about where some of those thoughts might come from such as media, peer teasing or upbringing. You don't have to blame yourself for this.
- **Self-kindness.** Try to replace your self-criticism with the same care you'd show a friend. Catch your self-talk and try and change it. If you were your own best friend, what would you say or do for you?
- **Realise your struggles are shared.** We can feel isolated in our struggles, believing our insecurities are unique. It's important to recognise that many concerns are universal, including appearance worries. This recognition can help reframe our own body dissatisfaction as a widespread issue rather than a personal flaw and reduce feelings of shame.

'I feel fat'— how to combat a bad body image day

Have you ever said 'I feel fat' to yourself, and how does it feel to call your body a name that has so many negative associations to it? Calling your body a nasty name and putting it down makes us feel ashamed of our bodies. It's disrespectful and cruel. Think of the schoolyard where when kids are being mean they call someone fat.

The word 'fat' is loaded with negativity and comes from an appearance-obsessed society that stigmatises people based on their body weight, size and shape. It comes from a society that tells us what a body should and shouldn't look like. We take this on board and are cruel to our bodies by the language we use towards it. I specialise, through my research and clinical work, in trying to understand why we think the way we do about our bodies and why we give in to diet culture and idealise unattainable bodies. Research shows that it's important to appreciate and respect our bodies and ourselves for good mental health.

Let me pass some tips.

First, 'fat' is not a feeling, it's a response to an emotion we have about something else. When we say we feel 'fat', it's often triggered by sadness, guilt, anger or anxiety over something that's happened. For example, we are having a hard time at work or school or with our friends and we turn this onto our body. It can be triggered by bodily changes that occur due to hormones, wearing tight clothing or something we've eaten.

Fat is a nasty word; it's used to be cruel and to punish. Unless you've done something really morally wrong, why do we need to be punished? Ask yourself this if you catch yourself being harsh towards your body. Eating is a common trigger where people judge themselves for eating something they think they shouldn't. This is diet brainwashing. But all food is good food, and no foods are morally better than others.

Work out what triggered this negative self-talk. Are you tired or feeling unhappy about something and that's making you take it out on your body? Have you been looking at unhelpful social media or websites about people's bodies? If so, think about changing this.

Treat your body like your best friend. You don't call your friend 'fat' or nasty names so don't do this to yourself. Learning to appreciate your body for what it can do as well as rejecting social and media pressures to look a certain way really helps improve your body image.

Your body will never be perfect as perfection doesn't exist. But your body deserves to be treated with respect, always.

Tackling weight stigma

I am a strong advocate for promoting respect for our bodies. Part of respecting our bodies involves being respectful of others' bodies. Weight stigma, where we talk negatively about a person's size and shape, is a common occurrence in our society. It leads many to develop poor self-esteem, anxiety around being in public, being judged and avoidance of eating in front of others.

There's a misperception that we can tell how healthy a person is by their body size, shape and weight, this is false. I work with many people who would be classified, through their BMI, as overweight or obese — conditions we are taught to view negatively — and yet can be incredibly healthy. In reverse, those who are seen as 'thin' must be healthy, which is not always the case. A person's health is defined as being absent from disease and in a state of wellbeing. This is measured by internal health including that of our brain, organs and heart, bone and skin, as well as how fit we are and many other ways. An important part of our health status is our mental health, where our state of wellbeing can be measured by stress and anxiety levels, mood, sleep quality, engagement in pleasure and enjoying our lives. We can have all this despite body size, weight or shape. Think of the most optimistic person you know or someone you would describe as happy — I bet their appearance has got nothing to do with this.

How do we reduce weight stigma?

Judgements about people's appearance are made all the time, but even a so called 'compliment' can be received negatively. I see clients who have been told many times that they're attractive or beautiful, yet they don't feel that way or it makes them feel self-conscious or concerned that's all people see them for. We need to stop commenting on people's weight and appearance and making this a source of value judgement, think about the whole person. What do you love about them in terms of their qualities, values and traits? Our appearance changes all the time, think about those you love and why you love them — it's not about what they look like, is it?

Stop the diet talk. What a boring subject it is; talking about what diet we are on and what we are depriving ourselves of. What about talking about our experiences and interests? What we think about the issues of the world or holidays we might be planning. We can also talk about food for its function rather than making moral judgements about the marketing of 'good' foods and 'bad' foods. Where did we get these ideas from and are they actually true?

How to stop that chocolate guilt

Feeling guilty about overeating chocolate is not uncommon because it's associated with being a 'bad' food, something we 'should' restrict and not eat 'too much' of. It's not surprising then that people with eating disorders, those dieting and those with concerns around their bodies really struggle with this issue.

Why do you think chocolate is bad?

Ask yourself this question, where have you learnt this? Most likely from diet advertising and messages about foods that make you 'fat' (a horrible word). Perhaps you weren't allowed to eat it growing up or it was only for special occasions. We learn all the time negative messages about certain foods and what they will supposedly do to our bodies. Food is also used as a punishment or reward, but my dietician colleagues will tell you that all foods are 'good' foods and that's why we are encouraged to eat a variety of foods, including chocolate.

Labelling food

When we label something as bad or not good for us, we attach morals and values to that food and then feel bad for eating it. When we restrict our diet and what we allow ourselves to eat, it often leads to more cravings of the food. When we eat it, we are more likely to overeat or binge on it and then beat ourselves up for this behaviour.

Let go of judgement

I work with people struggling with attaching emotions to food and we work on letting go of judgement of ourselves and others eating. Food is just food, and all food helps us in some way, whether that's to fuel our body or make us feel pleasure. A healthy relationship with food leads to a more positive mindset about eating and ourselves. We need to learn to love and respect our bodies by eating a variety of foods and not depriving ourselves. For most people, if they allow themselves to eat what their body needs and wants, they can eat some chocolate, enjoy it, and then stop when they've had enough.

Body dissatisfaction

When we don't like our appearance, it often affects our eating, which leads us to deprive ourselves or punish our bodies. You have to learn to respect your body for all that it does for you. Your body has done nothing wrong, allow it to rest and enjoy itself, that includes eating yummy foods.

So enjoy your chocolate in moderation. Share it with friends and family over celebrations or simply as a treat. Savour the taste rather than eating it all at once.

Fostering positive body image

Have you ever listened to how you speak to your body? Do you talk about what you think is wrong with it and what you want to change about it? For example, my body is too fat or flabby. And how does it make you feel when you do this?

Unfortunately, feeling negative or dissatisfied with your body is a common occurrence, especially for young people. It's seen as 'normal,' for females in particular, to not like their weight, shape or size.

How we feel about our body can affect our mood, self-esteem, eating, engagement in exercise, socialising, romantic relationships and anxiety. In extreme cases, a person with a very negative body image can develop an eating disorder, a severe mental health condition that affects a person's mental and physical wellbeing.

The reason for this dissatisfaction comes from our internalisation of beauty ideals portrayed in the media around what weight, shape and size is seen as attractive for either gender. When we internalise these ideals, compare our bodies to them and see a difference, we often feel less happy with our own body.

Diet culture also has a lot to answer for where we are obsessed with weight loss, needing to be thinner, smaller, more toned or more muscular. We know, for example, that early dieting is a risk factor for an eating disorder, as well as teasing about our appearance and weight by peers and family. Sexual trauma can also make us feel bad about our bodies.

So, what can we do to feel better about our bodies? I use the analogy of talking to yourself like you are your best friend, someone you speak to with appreciation, respect and kindness. When we are respectful towards our body, we talk to it nicely, we feed it, we give it rest, we move it, and do fun things with it.

We can also reject media messages around 'idealised' bodies and rather celebrate diversity in appearance, including in what a 'healthy' body looks like. Unfollowing celebrities and social media sites that promote dieting and weight loss can help to reduce the impact of diet culture. Having a bit of a social media detox can offer relief and lessen the internalisation of negative body messages.

Think about your body and all the wonderful things it does. For example, my arms help me hug my children tightly. My bottom helps me sit comfortably at school. My tummy helps support my posture. My face makes people happy when I smile.

Accept compliments. We receive them all the time, when someone smiles at us, says it's nice to see us, compliments our outfit. When someone says something positive about you or your body, accept it, don't just shrug it off. Say 'thank you' and really think about the compliment. Write it down and store it for when you need a pick-me-up.

Part 3

Relationships, Connection, and Communication

Loneliness: Why it happens and how to feel more connected

Loneliness is something we all experience at some point in life, and I'm no exception. Even as a clinical psychologist, there have been times when I've felt disconnected or isolated, despite being surrounded by people. Loneliness isn't just about being alone — it's that deep feeling of not being emotionally connected to others. It can creep in during life changes, after a loss, or even when everything on the surface seems fine.

What many people don't realise is just how common loneliness is. I see it in clients of all ages — young adults trying to find their place in the world, people navigating breakups or career changes, and older adults who feel left behind. Despite how connected we are through social media, more people than ever report feeling isolated. Life transitions — moving to a new place, starting a new job, or simply drifting apart from friends — can make loneliness even more intense. And the longer it lasts, the harder it can feel to break free from.

Loneliness has many causes. Sometimes it's situational — maybe you've just moved and don't know anyone, or your friends are busy with their own lives. Other times it comes from within — self-doubt, social anxiety, or feeling like you're not 'enough' can make it hard to reach out. Have you ever hesitated to message a friend because you didn't want to seem needy? That thought occurs to many people. The modern world doesn't help either — remote work and more online interaction have all made it harder to form deep, real-life connections.

For single people, loneliness can feel even more noticeable. Society puts so much pressure on romantic relationships, making it seem like being in one is the only way to feel connected. But I remind my clients that connection isn't just about having a partner. Strong friendships, supportive family, and even small everyday interactions — like chatting with a neighbour or sharing a laugh with a colleague — can be just as meaningful.

But the good news is that loneliness isn't permanent. The first step is recognising it without judgement — it's a normal human experience, not a personal failing. Instead of focusing on how many people you have around you, think about the quality of your connections. A deep conversation with one person can be more fulfilling than a hundred social media interactions.

Finding activities that bring you joy — like exercise, creative hobbies, or volunteering — can also help. These not only improve your mood but often create opportunities to meet like-minded people. Even small steps, like reaching out to a friend or joining a group, can make a difference.

Most importantly, be kind to yourself. Loneliness can make you feel like you're not important or that no one cares, but that's not true. Everyone feels lonely at times, but with small, intentional changes, you can feel more connected, supported, and at peace in your own company.

How to recognise and deal with a manipulator

Manipulation is when someone uses sneaky or unfair tactics to influence or control you, often for their own benefit. It's a way of twisting situations, emotions, or facts to make you feel guilty, confused, or obligated to do what they want. It can occur in relationships, by family members and in the workplace. It has a detrimental effect on your confidence, your self-esteem and mental health. We often don't realise we are being manipulated so recognising manipulative behaviour is key to protecting your mental health and having healthy relationships.

Here are some common signs that someone might be trying to manipulate you.

They say one thing but do another. A manipulative person might promise to respect your boundaries but then repeatedly ignore them.

They make you doubt yourself (Gaslighting). They might deny things they said or make you feel like you're 'imagining things' to mess with your confidence.

They always play the victim. They'll twist situations to make themselves look helpless, saying things like, 'No one ever helps me,' so you feel guilty and step in.

They use your emotions against you. They might say things like, 'If you really cared, you'd do this for me,' to guilt or pressure you into doing what they want.

They give you the silent treatment. They stop talking to you or withhold affection to punish or control you.

They're overly charming. They might pile on compliments and flattery to win you over but use it later to get you to do something for them.

They involve others to try and control you (Triangulation). They might say things like, 'Everyone agrees you're overreacting,' to make you feel isolated or insecure.

What you can do

Firstly, trust your gut. If something feels off or you're always second-guessing yourself after interacting with someone, trust those feelings. Also, pay attention to patterns and notice if their behaviour happens repeatedly or if they often make you feel bad or unsure.

Set boundaries with the person and be clear about what you're okay with, like saying, 'I can't help you with this right now' and stick to your limits. Getting a second opinion by talking to a friend or family member about their experience of the person or talk to a psychologist to get an objective perspective.

Try to stay calm and focus on facts when you are dealing with the person Instead of reacting emotionally. Point out the truth calmly, like, 'You said you'd do this, but it didn't happen. Can we talk about why?'

Sometimes you must distance yourself from the person. If they don't stop manipulating you, consider limiting your time with them or cutting ties to protect yourself.

By recognising these signs and standing firm, you can handle manipulation and keep your relationships healthier and more balanced.

Navigating disagreements: How to engage in respectful conversations and avoid arguments

Disagreements are a natural part of life, whether with friends, family, or even strangers. While it can be tricky to engage with those who hold different views, handling these situations with patience, openness, and respect is key. By encouraging healthy conversation, we can express our opinions without creating unnecessary tension or conflict. Let's look at some common disagreements and how to handle them.

One area where disagreements often arise is in political discussions. Conversations about candidates, policies, or social issues can quickly heat up, especially when emotions get involved. For example, imagine you're at a family gathering, and a relative is a strong supporter of a political figure you don't agree with. Instead of jumping into a heated argument or trying to convince them they're wrong, take a step back and ask open-ended questions. Phrases like

'What makes you feel that way?' or 'Can you explain why you support this?' can turn the conversation from a confrontation into a more understanding exchange. Even if you still don't see eye to eye, both sides can walk away with a better understanding of where the other person is coming from, making the discussion more respectful.

Disagreements also often pop up in personal relationships, such as with close friends or a partner. When making decisions, whether it's planning a holiday, dealing with a big life change, or choosing what to have for dinner, it's easy to think the other person is wrong. However, everyone's opinions are shaped by their own experiences and values, and we need to respect this. So instead of focusing on proving you're right, try listening actively. For example, reflect on what you've heard, such as 'I understand why you'd feel that way' or 'I see how you came to that conclusion'. This shows that you respect their point of view, even if you don't agree. This keeps the conversation cooperative and ensures both voices are heard.

Even in casual, day-to-day chats, like debating the best way to spend the weekend or what's the best type of food, disagreements can be small but still provide an opportunity for respectful communication. Rather than letting small differences escalate into an argument, approach them with a bit of humour or curiosity. Asking questions like 'What do you like about that?' or 'Why do you prefer that?' can keep the conversation light and fun. These moments can remind us that it's the variety in opinions that make our interactions more interesting.

At the end of the day, the key to navigating disagreements is to avoid turning them into arguments and instead focus on understanding. You don't need to 'win' or convince others they're wrong to have a meaningful chat. The goal is to listen patiently, stay open-minded, and respect the other person's view. By approaching differences with empathy and curiosity, you can maintain strong relationships and turn disagreements into opportunities for learning and growth, without the need to argue.

How to spot your friendship soulmate

Notice I said friendship soulmate? When we think of what a soulmate is we often think of it in a romantic sense, but I want to talk here about those friends we have that are our friendship soulmates.

Our soulmate friend is someone we feel connected to in a way that is more significant and profound than with any other person and we might have several. It can feel almost like something higher than ourselves has brought this person into our life. They're that person who you might not have seen or spoken to in ages but as soon as you talk to them, it's like you just spoke yesterday. They're the person you can just talk about anything with including what's relevant right here, right now, no need to re-cap since you last spoke. Despite how far away they might be, perhaps they're an overseas friend, it never stops you from connecting. They're that person who when you see something funny you want to tell them about it because you know they'll find it funny too or at least they'll join in with your enthusiasm.

Our soulmate friend is the one that may have known us for years and yet the connection is just as strong over the years. Despite changes in jobs, relationships, kids and mental health challenges, you've stayed just as close even if you might not have seen them in years. You understand each other and you often know the right things to say to each other to cheer each other up and be supportive. They get your sense of humour and they know how you'll respond to something.

Soulmates are often described as a friendship that is just simple and easy. Someone you don't have to try hard with. It's never a struggle with this person and you're comfortable being silent in each other's company when it's needed. It's no effort.

This person always supports you, no matter how crazy your ideas are. They help you grow as a person and are there in good times and bad. Perhaps you met them at just the right time in your life when you really needed them, or you met them at the strangest time like while travelling or at a party.

Your soulmate finds your quirkiness endearing and they can laugh with you when you tell them about things that irritate you.

You miss them when they're not around and are so happy just to hear their voice or receive a message from them just to say hi or check in. They accept you unconditionally and you love them.

So, who's yours? They might be a childhood friend, someone you used to work with, a family friend. If you haven't found yours yet, they're out there. Don't stop looking as they'll likely show up when you least expect them, and you'll know instantly when you've found them.

Psychologically healthy friendships are worth investing in

Friendships at any age are important for our mental health. When healthy, they can provide a sense of belonging, security, happiness, fun and adventure, add value to our life and make us feel good about ourselves. Healthy friends also encourage us to live well and want good things for us. They are there for both the good and the bad.

When we have an unhealthy friendship with someone, they can be extremely damaging to our mental and physical health. Think about that friend who always lets you down, is never there for you, only ever talks about themselves, makes you do things you don't want to do, or gets you into trouble at school or with your family.

You might have a toxic friend who you know isn't good for you, but you stay with them out of 'loyalty' or because you've known them for a long time or you feel guilty about letting them go. Unhealthy friends don't make you feel good about yourself — you often feel lonely in the friendship, judged, or like you can't trust them or go to them when you need them.

So how do you break up with a friend who isn't good for you?

You have to look after yourself and your interests and be okay with letting someone go. Distancing yourself from the friend or being brave and having a conversation with them about your thoughts and feelings might be needed. Get support from others if you're finding it hard to detach. Empathise with their feelings but be firm about your decision.

Alternatively, how do you deal with being ditched as a friend by someone else?

This can be especially painful when someone you've been friends with for a long time or you thought your friendship was solid stops contacting you or including you in their life.

It's okay to be hurt and sad, we have to grieve the loss of our friend, just like the loss of anything else. Seek out support from others and assess why the friendship ended. Was it because you've both grown apart or you don't have anything in common with each other anymore perhaps? Talk to someone about how you're feeling and plan to do something that helps you feel valued and loved such as being around family, pets or your community. We often think it's our fault and it might not be.

Without friends we feel lonely, so work out how to make new friends and connections. Give it time, as it takes time to build up new friendships. It also requires effort so be willing to try new things and open yourself up to new people. You could meet new people through a hobby, joining an interest group, volunteering, reaching out to neighbours or starting a conversation with someone you see regularly but have never spoken to.

Friendships require nurturing from both parties and are worth investing in.

The psychological benefits of being single

This is for all those single people out there experiencing pity from their partnered friends and constantly being set up or asked why they're single. Those well-meaning friends who have someone who's 'just right for you' or think the answer to your happiness is finding the right partner. I counsel plenty of single clients who are sick and tired of being asked, often by family, when they're going to get married as if that is the answer to ultimate happiness.

There are many myths out there that single people are lonely and unfulfilled. There's also social and cultural pressure to settle down and get married. It's often the first question adults get asked; Are you married? Well, let's take a look at the science of the benefits of being single, shall we?

Studies on people who are single by choice have actually shown that they are often more confident in themselves in terms of who they are, their values and what's important to them. They have time to prioritise their own needs, pursue goals and hobbies and are often better at self-care (think of relaxation and sleep) and looking after themselves.

Many people who have been single for a significant period of time by choice are comfortable in their own skin, they know who they are and often don't waste time with those people who suck energy from them. Rather, they have quality relationships with friends who lift them up and support them. Single people can also often be more generous to others with their time and are often seen as kind and caring by their friends and colleagues. Long-term singles often know themselves well and if they do decide to start a relationship, they're often more secure in themselves and clearer about their needs and their response to the needs of others.

Of course, we all need to feel connected to people, but this doesn't have to be through a romantic relationship. If we have good quality relationships with family, friends and colleagues, this provides us with a feeling of being understood, cared for, loved and appreciated.

There's also plenty of research on the detrimental effects to our mental health if we are in the wrong relationship. Think of those in relationships, whether romantic or not, that are disrespectful and unloving, or those where a person feels they've lost the sense of who they are or they feel lonely within the relationship.

Whether single or not, good mental health involves respecting yourself and others and having quality relationships with others which can occur in many forms. It's about prioritising your needs and looking after yourself. So single people, next time you're asked the question about whether you're in a relationship, you can say 'Yes, I'm in a fabulous one with myself!'.

Share the excitement: The psychological importance of joining in

We've all experienced being excited. That frenetic rush of adrenaline and feeling of positive emotions that might make us yell for joy or jump up and down. It can also be that nervous energy; you cannot concentrate on anything else in anticipation of something really positive that's about to happen. You might feel it in anticipation of a baby being born, your favourite sporting team winning or looking forward to doing something fun with friends.

Excitement is a whole-body experience where we get a surge of adrenaline and a desire to act. That's what makes us jump up and down or talk quickly. This body excitement is what makes people loud and boisterous sometimes.

The best excitement is when others join in on our enthusiasm and share with us our emotions. Psychologists sometimes call this validation, where someone acknowledges how we feel and shares this with us. We all need to feel validated, that our experiences and our emotions are important and ok. This validation occurs even when the other person has no idea why we might be excited about something but joins in on it anyway. For example, when we might be excited about something we've bought or something we are doing, and the person shares our smiles and acknowledges that we're happy.

We share excitement all the time such as at sporting events with others where we all cheer on our team or the excitement of a crowd when the fireworks are going off. It feels good to share it with others.

Watching someone get excited often increases our enthusiasm for something, like when we watch a motivational speaker talk excitedly about a topic. It fuels us to act. It's used a lot in the workplace to try and increase productivity by eliciting positive emotions and motivation.

On the flipside, when we observe someone who isn't sharing in our excitement and enthusiasm, it can sap our energy and stop us from feeling positive. It can affect our decision-making and de-motivate us. We feel invalidated and that our emotions are not important, or we feel we are being silly or overreacting.

Children especially need the adults in their lives to share in their excitement and validate what's important to them and when they enjoy it. We need friends to share our passions with us, showing empathy and understanding.

Feeling excited all the time though does take its toll and can stop us from relaxing. It's very hard to be calm, relax and sleep well when something exciting is coming up. Which is why children can't sleep the night before Christmas! It also explains why our devices can be unhelpful at bedtime. We might see something or do something that gets us excited, and this isn't conducive to sleeping. Sometimes we need time to settle, re-focus on something calming and schedule the continuation of excitement for another day.

The psychological importance of celebrating birthdays

Do you look forward to your birthday every year or is it filled with dread? Whether we're excited by it or not has a lot to do with our personality, our age, our mental health and the people in our lives.

When we celebrate our birthday or the birthday of someone else, especially a child, we are essentially celebrating ourselves and our specialness. It is a day of affirmation for our existence in the world by, and with, those who care about us. It's about celebrating our uniqueness and contribution to the world. Acknowledgement and validation of our birthday, especially by others, can make us feel good about ourselves and loved by others, and help us feel purposeful and valued.

Children usually get very excited about their birthday, loving the special attention from others, the playing and gift-giving. Milestone birthdays for young people often signify changes in identity and have a special meaning such as turning 16 or 18 years old. The excitement over milestone birthdays can be the case at any age. Think of those turning 80 where the celebration reminds them of their social connections and reflections on achievements and memories over the years. However, research has shown that for some, birthdays can be accompanied by negative emotions where a person may reflect on losses and perceptions of a life missing of achievements or not feeling one is where they should be for their age.

For some, they don't want to celebrate their birthday or find that the social pressure to celebrate is overwhelming, especially for introverts. Sometimes there's disappointment that someone forgot your special day or for children and young people, that their friends might be away or unable to come to their party. There can also be a lot of pressure to be 'happy' on your birthday, even though your life circumstances might not be so good at that time.

So as a loved one, what do I do for someone who doesn't want to celebrate their birthday?

It's important to acknowledge that it's a person's birthday and that you're thinking of them and you care about them. But you can keep your birthday wishes and planning low-key if it's your partner and family member's birthday for example. You could plan a very small gathering with the person's very close friends and family and involve them in that planning so it's not a surprise that overwhelms them. It's best to avoid organising a surprise party for someone who is quite introverted or who gets socially overwhelmed easily. Maybe think about organising an activity for the person you know they would enjoy, that they can do alone or with just you.

By understanding your needs and wants and of those around you, you can find a comfortable way to appreciate this special annual celebration. So, find your own, comfortable way to celebrate being uniquely you.

Part 4

Children, Adolescents, and Family Life

How to talk to teens about alcohol

As a clinical psychologist, I have many parents, and their teens, come to me and ask questions about alcohol use and mental health. Talking to teens about alcohol can be challenging, but it's important to have open, honest, informed and calm discussions. Here are some tips, grounded in research, for parents.

Create a judgment-free space. Teens are influenced by their friends, and they may shut down if they feel judged. Avoid lecturing and instead ask open-ended questions like, 'What do you think about drinking?' or 'Have you ever felt pressured to drink?' Listening without reacting with anger or fear can help you build trust. If they mention what their friends are doing, use it as an opportunity to guide, not scold.

Explain the effects of alcohol. Many teens don't fully understand how alcohol affects their bodies and brains. The teenage brain is still developing, particularly in areas responsible for decision-making, impulse control and memory. Drinking alcohol during this time can interfere with this development, leading to long-term effects. It also impairs judgment, which can increase the likelihood of risky behaviour, like accidents or unsafe choices. While alcohol may seem like a way to relax, it can worsen anxiety and mood swings over time. Helping teens understand this can guide them toward healthier coping strategies.

Be a positive role model. Teens often mimic adult behaviours, so it's important to model responsible drinking. If they see you drinking responsibly, or not drinking at all, they are more likely to follow your lead. Reinforce that alcohol is a choice, not a necessity and that socialising doesn't always involve drinking. Share with them how you manage stress without turning to alcohol, for example.

Help them handle peer pressure. One concern many parents have is how to help their teens navigate peer pressure around drinking. Instead of providing alcohol for parties (which research shows increases drinking and risky behaviour), help them prepare for social situations. Teens can have a simple response ready, like 'No thanks, I'm good.' They can also bring their own non-alcoholic drink or plan an exit strategy if they feel uncomfortable. Role-playing these situations with your teen can help them feel confident and equipped to handle peer pressure.

Talk about consequences. Teens need to understand that drinking is not just about health, it can affect relationships, trust and future opportunities. Underage drinking can lead to legal problems, damage friendships, and affect things like school or job prospects. Instead of scaring them with consequences, talk to them about real-life risks and help them make informed decisions.

Keep the conversation going. Talking about alcohol isn't a one-time conversation. Keep checking in, asking how they're feeling, and maintaining open communication. The more teens feel supported, the more likely they are to come to you with questions or concerns. Creating an ongoing, open dialogue about alcohol will help your teen make healthier decisions and feel more confident in social situations.

Being yourself and making friends: A guide for adolescents

Adolescence can be a confusing time, especially when you're trying to figure out who you are and how to connect with others. As a clinical psychologist, I've seen many young people face these challenges, so here's a simple guide to help you be yourself and make lasting friendships.

First, it's important to understand who you are. Adolescence is a time of self-discovery, and you might not have everything figured out just yet — and that's completely normal. Take the time to explore what excites you, whether it's music, art, or sports. It's okay to change and grow as you discover more about yourself.

Building confidence and self-esteem is essential for making friends. When you feel good about who you are, it's easier to connect with others. You might experience moments of self-doubt, but try focusing on what makes you unique. Celebrate your strengths, whether it's being a good listener or having a talent for solving problems.

Acknowledge these qualities and be kind to yourself, especially when things don't go perfectly.

Making friends involves communication, so it's important to practice talking to others. Start with small conversations that feel comfortable, and with time, it will get easier. Ask about people's hobbies, interests, or favourite activities. These simple conversations often lead to deeper connections. You don't need to say anything perfect; just be yourself and let the conversation flow naturally.

Building strong friendships takes time and trust, so take it slowly. Share personal things gradually and let connections grow naturally. If a friend is upset or struggling, empathise with them by saying things like, 'I'm sorry you're struggling' or 'I'm here if you need me'. This helps create deeper bonds without rushing things.

Setting healthy boundaries is also important. Knowing when to say 'no' and protecting your time and energy helps ensure your relationships remain balanced. If you're feeling tired or overwhelmed, it's okay to turn down plans. Putting yourself first when needed keeps friendships healthy and respectful.

Body image is another important part of adolescence. Many young people struggle with how they look, but it's important to remember that your worth is not determined by your appearance. Confidence comes from within. Focus on what makes you feel strong, healthy, and happy, and avoid comparing yourself to others. Self-love is essential for building meaningful, supportive friendships.

Becoming yourself and making friends takes time, patience, and practice. Understand who you are, focus on building confidence, and create healthy relationships.

And remember, asking for help along the way is okay. With time and self-compassion, you'll form the connections you deserve.

A mental health guide to helping your child transition back to school

I work with many families navigating the challenges of returning to school, starting a new school or starting school for the very first time. This transition can bring mixed emotions for children and parents. Parents play a critical role in helping their children feel confident and ready for a school year ahead.

Start by creating a safe space for your child to express their feelings. Acknowledge that it's normal for children to feel excited, nervous, or uncertain about school. Let your child know that these feelings are okay and reassure them that many kids feel the same way. Listening with empathy and providing support can ease their worries.

The idea of going back to or starting school can feel overwhelming. Instead of focusing on the whole school year, help your child break down the transition into smaller, more manageable steps such as focusing on one day at a time. When it comes to assessments for older children, help them work on manageable, small steps and reassure them that you are there to support them.

Establishing a consistent routine is crucial. Children thrive on structure, and a predictable daily routine provides stability. I know this can be hard but try and start the day with a calming morning routine for everyone in the home. A consistent evening routine, ensuring good sleep hygiene, is just as important. Proper rest supports mental wellbeing and helps children manage stress during the day. It can be hard to stick to routines, especially during stressful periods and with the distractions of social media, but consistency creates comfort and predictability for your child.

It's also essential to communicate with your child's school. Teachers and support staff are there to help and may offer accommodations like extra breaks or quiet spaces if needed. Stay in touch with the school to ensure your child has the support they require. This collaboration helps create a positive school experience. Knowing the school is aware of your child's needs can provide peace of mind.

Encouraging healthy habits is key to supporting your child's emotional resilience. Ensure they are eating nutritious meals, staying active, and making time to relax. Physical activity can help reduce anxiety, while a balanced diet provides the energy needed to focus and stay alert. By developing these habits, you help your child build the mental strength they need to face challenges.

Watch for any signs that your child may be struggling. If they seem withdrawn, irritable, or unusually tired, it could indicate stress or anxiety. Gently check in with them and create an open environment where they feel comfortable sharing. If these symptoms persist, consider seeking professional support to help your child cope. Acting early can prevent issues from escalating.

Finally, remember to care for yourself as a parent. Parenting through transitions can be stressful, so prioritise self-care. When you look after your own mental wellbeing, you'll be better able to support your child. I know it can be hard to make time for yourself, but doing so will help you stay strong for your child.

Taking a gap year: The pros and cons for young people and parents

I work with many young adults who are finishing Year 12 and considering whether to take a gap year. I also teach students who come to university straight after school and those who have taken a year off. Additionally, I support parents who often feel uncertain about their child's decision to take a break, wondering if an entire year is necessary and how to ensure it's a productive experience.

From a psychological perspective, a gap year can offer significant mental health benefits, particularly for young people who have experienced stress or burnout during their final school years. A break from academic pressures can help them reset emotionally and mentally, reigniting their enthusiasm for study or work. This time away often allows them to return with a renewed sense of focus and motivation.

A gap year can also be an opportunity for personal growth and self-discovery. It provides a chance to reflect on life goals, explore interests, and mature before diving into further studies or a career. Many young people choose to travel, which exposes them to new cultures and broadens their worldview. Learning to adapt to different environments and manage independently can be incredibly valuable. Those who combine travel with work often gain practical skills, learn how to budget, and may even pick up a new language. For others, volunteering during this time enhances transferable skills like communication and teamwork.

Of course, there are challenges associated with taking a gap year. Travel can be expensive, and delaying education or employment has financial and personal opportunity costs. Postponing studies or work can impact long-term goals, such as earning a degree, starting a career, or saving for independence. Additionally, stepping away from structured environments for an extended period can make it harder to return to academic or professional routines. Some young people I've worked with have expressed feeling 'left behind' when they return from a gap year and see their peers advancing in their studies or careers.

To help young people make the most of a gap year, I emphasise the importance of planning. Setting clear goals and creating a structured plan — thinking through where to go, how long to stay, and who to travel with—can make a huge difference. I often remind them that they don't need to take the full year off. Sometimes, a few months is enough to achieve their goals and recharge. Budgeting wisely and saving in advance is essential, as is choosing cost-effective and meaningful activities. Staying connected with family and friends provides much-needed support, especially when travelling. I also stress the importance of self-care — getting enough rest, eating well, and being mindful of safety are critical to enjoying the experience.

For parents, I encourage open communication. Know where your child is, help them with budgeting, and have a contingency plan in case things don't go as expected. A gap year doesn't have to last 12 months; options like mid-year university entry or a short break over summer may be just as effective.

With careful planning, a gap year can be a life-changing experience, but it requires forethought to maximise the rewards and minimise the risks.

Dealing with body image issues in the lead up to the school formal

I see many young clients with body image issues where they hold negative perceptions of their appearance; they're the wrong body shape or weight, aren't attractive enough, or they don't look good enough. This can lead many to feel unhappy about themselves and also into dangerous behaviours such as dieting for weight loss, excessive spending on makeup and clothing to 'look their best' and anxiety leading up to the event.

Young people face a lot of pressure from social media and their peers regarding their appearance, including weight, skin, hair, shape, and size. We hear people being teased for their appearance and teens are more susceptible to falling for the traps of marketing to buy products or do things to look a certain way with the promise of it bringing happiness.

The school formal is meant to be a time of celebration. Where young people get together with their friends, enjoy a lovely day and evening, maybe for the last time in their schooling. For many though, it's met with dread and anxiety. It's a particularly dangerous time for those with eating disorders, so I will talk here about how to help your teen at this time.

Firstly, try to shift the focus away from appearance. We know that it's not as simple as saying 'it doesn't matter what you look like' to a teen, but as adults, we should avoid overemphasising appearance. When shopping for an outfit, make it a pleasant experience and try to stay away from making comments about weight, shape and size. Instead, comment on how they look happy and comfortable. When they're doing their make-up and hair, comment on their talents around this. Ask them about their friends and what they'll do to have fun. Comment on how proud you are of them for who they are.

Look out for signs of concern, such as your child not eating or talking about the effects of foods on their body. Instead, focus on talking about food in terms of its function—how it provides energy and supports mood and relaxation. Avoid conversations about dieting or making comments about your own body and eating habits, as this helps to model a positive body image.

Focus on other things that are going on in your teen's life. What else are they doing and enjoying? Try not to buy into the need for everything to be just right for the event but rather enjoying the lead up and focusing on other priorities.

Talk to your teen. Ask them what they're worried about and why and ask them if they want to talk to someone. Remember, it's just one event that will come and go quickly.

Body image in young people: How do we help them?

Body image refers to a person's perception of their body (what we think it looks like, which might not be based on reality), and our attitudes and feelings towards it (whether we like it or not and how respectful we are towards it). Research by the Butterfly Foundation (the National Eating Disorder Organisation) on youth aged 12–18 years found that body dissatisfaction (having negative attitudes, perceptions and feelings towards your body) occurred for more than half of young people of all gender identities and sexual preferences. So, body dissatisfaction is not just a female issue as commonly thought.

Young people said that social media had a negative impact and so did being teased for their appearance. It made many of them not want to go to school and avoid socialising or bringing attention to themselves.

This is not new information. We've known for a long time about the impact of poor body image on mental health, particularly the development of eating disorders. Poor body image can affect anyone at any age in a way that makes them feel bad about themselves and anxious. It impacts our relationship with food and exercise. I work with people of all ages where their body image impacts on their life in a negative way.

In my, and my students' research at the University of Canberra, we look at not only the negative side of social media's impact on body image but also the benefits, including what we can learn from those with a positive body image. What we've found is that focusing on the function of your body, what it can do rather than what it looks like, makes you feel better about it and yourself. Also, expressing gratitude towards your body, including talking to it nicely rather than berating it.

We have also found that social media breaks are important, especially when young people constantly compare themselves to others they perceive as having better looks or better lives. In their study, The Butterfly Foundation found that for about 60 per cent of young people, social media made them feel unhappy with their bodies and sometimes not want to engage in life. Taking a break from social media often stops this unhelpful comparison and engages the young person in their life.

As adults, we need to be role models to our young people by respectfully talking about ourselves and others and engaging in activities that lift us up rather than pull us down. Teasing and bullying are not ok, and we can empower our young people to speak up for themselves and their friends. Unfortunately, most of us have experienced times when we've been teased, and it feels awful. Offer validation for feelings and non-judgement when someone comes to you with their worries.

Fathering: The toughest job in the world

Let's take a moment to reflect on what it means to be a father. It's not just the male who donated their sperm or happened to be related to you, but the man who's your dad, the one who loves you unconditionally and has your very best interests in mind. Who does more than just provide the finances or the house but the one who tries his best to meet our emotional and psychological needs. There's no one-size-fits-all father, and all have their strengths and weaknesses, they are only human after all, and they learn as they go. They have to adapt as we age and go through changes, and they learn about us through our mistakes and triumphs.

Our relationship with our biological father can be complex. Not all fathers are cut out to be fathers and not all great father figures are related to us. Perhaps there's a father figure in your life who you can always go to, who looks after you, and supports all your adventures, hopes and dreams. They might be someone who's practically helpful and provides financial support but is also there to support your emotional needs. Your father figure is someone you feel proud to call your dad despite their limitations and annoying habits.

When psychologists talk about positive fathering, it's not about being perfect or never getting cross or disappointed. But it's about being present in your child's life no matter how old they are. It's about being engaged with your child through listening, understanding, validating and having unconditional positive regard if when they make mistakes. It's about looking out for your child's mental health needs through emotional support or helping them find this if it's beyond your expertise. A good father doesn't have to be rich in finances, but they do need to provide not just the basics of care (food, shelter, schooling, medical needs) but help ensure their child knows they are there for them in good times and bad. They aren't cruel and they don't put their children down even when teaching right from wrong. Dads set reasonable boundaries, and a child finds them predictable and stable.

Children's self-esteem and ultimate wellbeing are maximised when a father knows how to get help if they don't know what to do, they encourage help-seeking and are proud of their child and who they are even though they may do things that are disappointing.

Being a father is a tough job that requires dedication and a willingness to do their best. However, it's also okay for dads to ask for help, admit when they are struggling, and not be perfect. In fact, showing imperfection and making mistakes is an important lesson for children.

Being a dad is one of the hardest and most important jobs, with no instruction manual. Dads learn to adapt to the unique needs of each child.

The psychology of being a mother

When a woman becomes a mother, it is a psychologically transformative experience. A woman's identity is changed in an instant when she becomes a mother and her life often changes in ways she never expected. For some women this transformation is smooth and easy but for many it's not. There's a reason why it's called the hardest job in the world and a mother never stops learning or doing her job. I note that not everyone has a mother who gave birth to them in their life. Here when I talk about the importance of the mother, I mean the person who cares and loves their child in an unconditional and empathic way that is unlike any other.

I have many clients who ask me 'What's a good mother and how do you know if you're a good mother or you have a good mother?'. From a psychologist's point of view, a good mother is one who loves her child unconditionally and can meet their emotional needs. She's accepting of who her child is and she's responsive to her child, she allows her child to make mistakes and forgives. Unfortunately, motherhood is often portrayed in the media and culturally in ways that are unrealistic and in an idealised view, putting a lot of pressure on mothers. A good mother isn't perfect, she makes errors of judgement and sometimes gets angry and frustrated but she's loving and always has the best interests of her child in mind. She doesn't have to treat all of her children the same but rather interacts with them depending on their individual needs and loves them all equally.

Children need reassurance, touch, and unconditional love, and mothers (and mother types) intuitively know this. Mothers will often say their connection with their child happened instantly but for some, it can take more time. Sometimes a mother may be struggling with her own mental health. For example, in cases of post-natal depression, the mother really wants to feel connected to her child but for some reason cannot. This is where mothers need to seek out support for themselves from a non-judgemental person like a psychologist. There are also times when a mother may not like her child because they've made her cross, so learning parenting tips can help too.

Children don't come with their own instruction manual, so mothers are learning as they go and making mistakes all the time. Often how a mother was mothered herself influences her behaviour and I work with many women who don't want to mother like they were mothered. Mothering also changes as a child ages so she can be filled with different anxieties over time.

Mothers are busy, often taking care of several children, taking care of the home and the office. They need to support and love themselves as well as time to look after their own needs.

Why won't they ask for help? Helping the men in your life seek help

Did you know that one in five men suffer from an anxiety disorder at some stage in their life and that depression occurs in about one in eight men? Post-Traumatic Stress Disorder and Substance Abuse Disorders are also common. Yet men seeking help, especially older men, is not common. They often suffer in silence or can be seen to be suffering by those around them but won't seek help. I talk to a lot of parents and partners in my practice about their concerns about their loved ones who are reluctant (or outwardly refuse) to seek help.

One of the biggest reasons why it is difficult for some men to ask for help is they do not want to be perceived as a burden to their friends and family. Just like anyone, men can think that they are putting someone out when they ask for help. But the help, from professionals especially, is there for a reason, because there's a need. Also, people in your life generally ask if you're ok or whether they can help because they want to. Not getting help, when others can see you're struggling, is actually more of a worry for your loved ones.

Seeking help from a psychologist for mental health issues can be especially challenging where a person perceives it to be a sign of weakness. But it's a strong and insightful person who asks for help. We educate our students at school and university about understanding our mental health, how to work on it, and seeking help early. We normalise seeking help for our mental health just like asking for any other type of help.

Sometimes men can have difficulty expressing their emotions and worry about verbalising how they feel. That old attitude of 'manning up' and 'getting on with it' is old school. Help seeking in young males is much more common as it's talked about more openly at school and in the home. School and university students for example, are strongly encouraged to seek help and deal with issues as they arise rather than putting worries off. Often there's a huge relief when someone gets mental health support because you're heard, listened to, respected, and you learn strategies to make yourself feel better.

A few things to consider when trying to help your loved one (whether that be your partner, relative or friend) who doesn't want help:

1. Listen and validate. Everyone needs to be heard and told it's ok.
2. Resist the urge to try and fix the problem or give advice.
3. Explore options together about where and who might be best placed to help.

4. Lead by example and take care of yourself and find your own support.

Part 5

Work, Change, and Life Transitions

Mental wellbeing in the workplace

We hear a lot about physical health and safety in the workplace, but you might not have heard of the term 'psychosocial safety'. Psychosocial safety is about the mental and emotional wellbeing of an employee and their right to feel safe, from a mental health point of view, in the workplace. Psychosocially safe workplaces are those where employees feel respected, supported, and valued, and are free from unnecessary stressors that harm a person's mental health. It's where a person has positive interactions with others, feels included and respected and secure in their employment.

As a clinical psychologist, I often hear about the mental health effects of workplaces that lack psychosocial safety. People affected describe environments where there may be excessive workloads, unrealistic deadlines, poor communication, and/or little social support. For example, some talk about feeling constant pressure to meet tight deadlines without adequate resources or acknowledgment, leaving them feeling unappreciated and burnt out. Others describe bullying and harassment creating a culture of fear and isolation. There may also be favouritism causing feelings of resentment. It's important to be able to recognise if you're in a psychologically unsafe workplace and take action to protect your mental health.

Some of these signs are physical and some emotional. Persistent feelings of stress, burnout, and physical symptoms such as headaches, fatigue, or insomnia often indicate an unhealthy environment. For example, you might dread work every morning, to the point of feeling physically unwell or even experiencing panic attacks. You might also feel isolated, anxious, or unable to trust colleagues. You might be working under a manager who dismisses concerns about your workload or fails to provide constructive feedback. Job insecurity and unclear expectations are also sources of stress. Employees unsure about their roles or worried about losing their jobs often feel on edge. This uncertainty can drive overworking to demonstrate value, which only exacerbates stress and exhaustion.

So, what do I do? When dealing with a psychologically unsafe workplace, it's essential to focus on what you can control. Setting boundaries is a critical first step. For instance, communicate your workload limits and establish clear expectations for working hours (i.e., not taking work home or being contacted outside of working hours). This protects your mental health and helps prevent burnout. Building a support network is also important such as connecting with trusted colleagues or sharing your experiences with friends and family. These conversations can reduce isolation and provide fresh perspectives. Prioritising self-care is also crucial including engaging in activities that help you unwind and recharge and take short breaks during the workday to help you manage stress and improve your focus. If the environment doesn't improve, document incidents like unreasonable demands or unprofessional behaviour to address the issues formally if needed. If it's really affecting you, consider professional support from a psychologist who can help you achieve a healthier work-life balance or perhaps move away from a toxic workplace.

Dealing with chronic stress in the workplace

I work with many clients experiencing stress due to workplace factors, including bullying and harassment, staff shortages, and under-resourcing of services, as well as working long hours. Some describe feeling chronically stressed both at work and at home.

What is stress?

Stress occurs when you perceive that the demands of your environment or what is expected of you outweigh your ability to cope, whether at work or at home. It is often an ongoing feeling of anxiety, trouble sleeping and eating, and mood changes such as being easily agitated or just feeling unmotivated to do anything. It often makes people withdraw from others and engage less in pleasurable activities. Stress also weakens the immune system, making a person more susceptible to illness and disease. For example, it can result in a longer recovery time from colds.

When I have worked with people experiencing workplace bullying and harassment, their stress often doesn't subside until they leave the workplace. This can be especially traumatic if the job provides them with a strong sense of meaning and purpose. It's important for a person to be supported in finding a healthier environment and also learn strategies to cope with workplace situations. Of course, it's crucial that workplaces are active in creating positive environments in the first place and take a no-tolerance approach to bullying. Bullying can have lifelong effects for some, leaving them unable to work due to the fear of being bullied again.

When the source of stress is removed or resolved (such as recovering from a loved one's illness or moving into a new home), or the person removes themselves from the stressful situation (such as leaving a job), there is often a sense of relief. However, the body may remain in a heightened state, taking time to recover. People often describe feeling unwell, experiencing headaches, muscle tension, and difficulty relaxing.

Set boundaries within your workplace

We need to set clear boundaries in the workplace in terms of how we are treated and the amount of work we take on. Learning to call out behaviour that is not acceptable as well as looking after our needs for breaks and manageable workloads is important but can be hard. Seeking support from supervisors and human resource departments can help.

Recovering from stress

It's important for a person to actively participate in relaxing activities to help their body and brain recover from a period of stress. However, sometimes a person may remain stressed, anticipating that the stressor (trigger) will return. In these cases, seeking help is important to learn ways to manage. Clinical psychologists often help people learn to relax, be more present during pleasant events, improve sleep and develop more helpful ways of thinking.

Navigating redundancy

Experiencing redundancy can be emotionally overwhelming, evoking feelings of anger, loss, uncertainty, and diminished self-esteem. From my perspective as a clinical psychologist, I recognise the profound impact this change can have on your career, mental health, and sense of identity. Let's talk about some strategies to support you during this transitional phase.

Firstly, it's important to acknowledge and validate your emotions. The emotional fallout of redundancy may include shock, frustration, anxiety, or grief — all of which are valid reactions. Allow yourself to experience these feelings without judgment. Expressing emotions by writing about them, confiding in trusted friends, or seeking professional help can provide clarity and foster healing. Suppressing these emotions may hinder your progress, so give yourself time and space to process them.

Reframe the situation. Although redundancy can feel personal, it is often a business decision unrelated to your skills or value. Viewing it as an opportunity for growth can be empowering. Reflect on questions like: *What have I gained from this role? What new possibilities are now open to me?* Such reframing can help shift your perspective from loss to opportunity, paving the way for a more fulfilling career or lifestyle.

Prioritise self-care. Losing a job can disrupt your routine, amplifying stress. Creating a new structure that includes activities promoting mental and physical wellbeing — such as exercising regularly, eating healthily, and maintaining good sleep hygiene — is crucial. Incorporating mindfulness practices like meditation or deep breathing can help alleviate anxiety and build resilience during this period too.

Address financial concerns. Financial uncertainty is a common source of stress after redundancy. Research available resources, such as severance pay or unemployment benefits, to alleviate immediate concerns. Crafting a clear financial plan can also help you regain a sense of stability and control.

Assess your skills and redefine your goals. This is an opportunity to reevaluate your career direction. Consider what aspects of your previous role brought you satisfaction and where you might seek change. Update your resume and explore opportunities to enhance your skill set or earn certifications that align with your ambitions. Setting small, realistic goals can provide focus and a sense of achievement.

Try to be patient and positive. Although redundancy is challenging, it is often a temporary phase. Building a new career path takes time, and setbacks are a natural part of the process. Be kind to yourself, celebrate small milestones — like completing a course or landing an interview — and maintain a forward-thinking attitude. This positivity can help strengthen your resilience and prepare you for future opportunities.

While redundancy may feel daunting, it can be an opportunity for growth and self-discovery. By focusing on self-care, seeking support, and approaching the situation proactively, you can transform this period of uncertainty into a chance for renewal and exploration.

Psychological health in retirement

Deciding to retire from work is a major decision, one which many spend years looking forward to with an idealised image of freedom to do what one wants, travel, take up hobbies and learn new things. It's our reward for all those years of hard work, contributions made to our families and society, and the sacrifices we've made. Most assume they're going to be happy and relaxed, free to do whatever they want.

But retirement for some people can be met with feelings of stress, anxiety and depression. Some may feel a loss of identity, loss of meaning or feel directionless. Some might feel isolated and lonely or may not have the money to do the things we want to enjoy. There can also be an expectation from adult children that we are now free and available to mind grandchildren or help with chores. It can also be a time when health might start to decline, and we worry about losing friends and family as we and they age.

So, what's the best way to have a fulfilling retirement? First of all, it's about planning for retirement, not just in a financial sense so we have the money to do the things we want, but also in terms of attitude and approach to life in retirement. It's ok to recognise that there will be things that we lose and miss, like socialising with our colleagues and a daily routine. People who have enjoyed their careers might feel sad and no longer valued. Some common questions are where, who and how can I get my needs met? For example, where will I get my social needs met? What is my identity in terms of what I'm interested in and what do I value? What will I do with my day?

Some things to think about are if you enjoy your work, do you need to retire completely? Or could you stay connected as a volunteer or do some part-time or unpaid work? What hobbies and new things could you learn? Are there new social or interest groups you could become a part of?

In retirement and generally, it's important to keep looking after your body and your health, including keeping your mind active to ward off ill health. If we haven't been so healthy during our working life, maybe now is the time to re-evaluate and make some changes. Staying physically active, practicing relaxation, doing things you enjoy, staying connected to others, thinking about what we're grateful for, setting a routine for the day and getting good sleep is important for everyone.

It is also important to talk to someone about your worries, whether that be a doctor, psychologist, financial planner, friends or family, so that your retirement is as relaxed and fulfilling as possible. Remember, this is your time to be you and to choose how and with whom you want to spend your time.

Busting the myths on ageing

How many times do you hear people talking about all the negatives of getting older or attributing a negative characteristic, such as being grumpy or slow, to someone because they're old? There are a lot of myths out there about ageing and older people, so let's bust a few of them.

I'm too old to change or learn something new

We always have the ability to learn something new, including how to use technology better, a second language, an instrument or complete a PhD! Learning something new takes patience and time which we often have more of when we're older.

Older people are lonely

Did you know that depression in older people is less common than in young people? Everyone can experience loneliness particularly when they lose friends, family and relationships but often older people have stronger and longer-lasting relationships and a lifetime of memories to think about and share with others. Often there's more time to catch up socially with family and friends when you're older as well as joining groups with like-minded people.

Everyone ends up in a nursing home

Only five percent of adults over 65 years of age live in a nursing home, and most older adults live independently. Whilst we often need more care as we get older, the majority of Australians live in their own homes.

Older people can't exercise because they might injure themselves

Studies have shown that we need to move our bodies at any age and that it's actually inactivity as we age that causes health concerns and injuries. Physical activity keeps our joints moving, our bones strong, our hearts beating, and leads to a longer life. Exercise is great for our mental health as it can relieve stress and can be social. Moving our bodies when we are older also helps improve our balance and stability and can help prevent falls and injuries.

Older people are grumpy

Older people are often happier than younger people. When asked, studies have found that older adults tend to describe their lives as enjoyable and less stressful compared to how they perceive younger people's lives today. It's understandable if you have health issues or are in pain that you'll be more irritable, but that's not an age thing. You can be irritable at any age — think of teenagers for example.

You lose your memory when you're older

Whilst they might have occasional incidents of forgetfulness, most older adults do not have significant declines in their memory. As we age, we accumulate more knowledge, have more experiences and more insights. Learning something new is a great way to keep our brains engaged and intact and many studies have found that our memory can improve if we keep challenging it with new things.

So, get out there and create new memories, new experiences and keep active.

If you are having concerns as you age, check in with your doctor to rule out anything serious and work on any strategies that can assist.

How to keep the holiday feeling going once you return home

Following a great holiday where we've been relaxed and shut off from the world and our worries, how do we keep that holiday feeling going when we return to work or school? It's not uncommon for people to go straight back to work after a holiday, getting straight back into the stress and hustle and bustle of everyday life only to feel the benefits of the holiday fade away within a week or two.

Take the first day slowly

Firstly, don't be too quick to pick up where you left off. Ease back into work, if you can, take a few days off when you return from a trip to ease back into daily life. Take things slowly. For example, on the first day back at work, set a simple goal like getting through the day and checking some of your emails. Don't try to achieve too much, or you'll be super stressed by the end of your first day back. Be realistic, your first day back will be tiring as your brain has been on holiday and isn't used to the sudden pressure.

Get good sleep, take your breaks, and finish on time, if not early.

Talk about your holiday

Talk about the fun you had on your holiday with colleagues and friends and show them your photos. Put your holiday souvenirs around your home and re-visit the fun you had with those you might have travelled with. This keeps the holiday 'alive' in your brain and its associated feelings. Imagine what you'd be doing if you were still on holiday and try to mimic this when you return. For example, you might keep reading your book, take more breaks, make time for a massage, wear comfortable clothes, go out for meals, and laugh.

Rewards

Have something nice to look forward to at the end of the first day and first week back at school and work, this can help with the post-holiday blues people can feel. Even planning your next trip can help keep you optimistic and set some things to look forward to in the near and distant future. Let people know if you're feeling jet-lagged or tired so they can be understanding. Don't overdo your appointments and schedule for week one.

Get lots of sleep

You might still be jet-lagged from your trip so go to bed early, get a good night's sleep and work on good sleep hygiene (relaxation before bed, getting back into a routine, eating regularly and adequately). It's important also to move your body and eat well to support your recovering body and brain after a week back into work or school.

So have an easy week back, keep the holiday feels alive and I hope you have another relaxing holiday coming up real soon.

Coping with Christmas from a mental health perspective

As Christmas and the end of the year approaches, many of us experience a mix of excitement and stress. The season brings warmth and togetherness, but it can also feel overwhelming. While the Christmas season is often joyful, it can also lead to pressure, anxiety, and sadness. The demands of shopping, planning gatherings, and navigating family dynamics can heighten stress. As a clinical psychologist, I'd like to share some practical tips to help you navigate this time of year more smoothly, allowing you to focus on what truly matters.

The Christmas season often comes with high expectations. Families may feel the need to create the 'perfect' celebration, leading to stress around gift-giving, event planning, and maintaining traditions. For those dealing with loss or change, these pressures can intensify feelings of sadness or loneliness. It's also important to recognise that it's perfectly okay not to celebrate Christmas at all. Everyone has their own beliefs and traditions, and choosing to opt out of festivities can be a valid way to prioritise your mental health.

Several factors contribute to Christmas stress

Financial strain can be significant, as the costs of gifts, decorations, and festive meals add up quickly. This can create anxiety, especially for those already struggling financially. The Christmas season is often packed with social obligations, from work parties to family gatherings, which can overwhelm you as you try to balance these commitments. Family dynamics can complicate things, bringing tensions to the surface, particularly if there are unresolved conflicts. The season can also evoke memories of lost loved ones or past disappointments, leading to feelings of grief or nostalgia.

Managing Christmas stress

Firstly, embrace realistic expectations. Understand that not everything has to be perfect. Setting achievable goals for yourself—such as how many events to attend or how much decorating to do—can ease pressure. Open communication with your family about expectations can foster a more relaxed atmosphere. For instance, if you usually host a large gathering but find it overwhelming this year, consider scaling back.

Self-care is crucial during the Christmas season. Make time for activities that uplift you, whether that's enjoying a quiet evening with a book, going for a walk, or practising relaxation techniques like deep breathing. Prioritising self-care helps balance the hustle and bustle.

The season can bring up a mix of emotions, especially if you're facing grief or loneliness. It's important to acknowledge and accept these feelings rather than push them away. If you feel overwhelmed, consider talking to someone you trust — a friend, family member, or psychologist. Sharing your feelings can provide relief and perspective. If you're feeling isolated, seek out opportunities to connect with others.

Coping with the lead-up to Christmas involves balancing expectations, prioritising self-care, and acknowledging your feelings. It's perfectly fine to focus on your wellbeing amidst the festivities — after all, Christmas is about connection and joy, but it's also okay to choose a path that feels right for you.

Preparing for SAD this winter

Seasonal Affective Disorder (SAD), is a depressive mental health condition that occurs for some people during the winter months. It's where, during the cold and dark period of the year, a person feels sad, unmotivated, low in mood and energy. They describe feeling down in the dumps and struggling to feel good about their life. Sleep is usually affected with people having trouble getting up and wanting to sleep a lot. For some, they can even feel so depressed they don't think they can keep living. Then when spring hits, their mood lifts and they feel ok again. SAD is a genuine condition and for those who suffer from it during the winter, it's a long period of time to feel like you're struggling.

What causes it?

We don't know exactly but we think that given it usually occurs during the winter, it's likely due to the fact that days are shorter and there's less light which disrupts our body's circadian rhythm and leads us to feeling down and depressed. The neurotransmitter serotonin (which plays a role in improving our mood) also drops when we have less sunlight. Winter also affects our melatonin levels, a hormone responsible for helping us sleep and may explain why we don't feel like getting up in the morning.

How do you prevent it?

Just like any form of depression, prevention and early intervention is best. Generally, what's good for our mood and mental health are:

- Having a regular routine of doing things you enjoy
- Doing social things with others and time with loved ones so you feel supported
- Moving your body and getting the blood pumping
- Trying to reduce our stress levels through regular relaxation and time out
- Getting good quality sleep by turning off devices and relaxing before bed
- Ensuring you're eating regularly and adequately
- Talking to someone about our worries and concerns

Specific SAD treatment

But in addition to generally looking after our mental health throughout the year, during the winter people with SAD should maximise their exposure to light and sun (in a sun-smart way of course). Getting vitamin D from sunlight helps us produce serotonin which is a neurotransmitter in our brain that improves our mood, that's how antidepressant medication often works. Also, try and get outside as much as possible exposing the brain to light to literally 'light it up' and get it feeling better. Put your winter woollies on and go for a walk in the fresh air and get a bit of sun on your face every day or for a few minutes a couple of times a day. Sit outside and have your lunch for example.

If you can, a nice holiday somewhere warm and sunny during our cold months can break up the winter blues.

Sick of being sick? How to cope psychologically when you're not well

When we are sick with a cold, flu or Covid, we can feel not only physically unwell but also irritable, anxious and sad. When unwell, people often describe feeling quite miserable and it can hit you all of a sudden. The reason why we feel this way is because when we are sick our immune system registers that it's under attack by a pathogen or toxin and needs to fight (that's how we get better). Unfortunately, the cells of our immune system also include our brain which is responsible for our emotions, actions and feeling fatigued. Our body and brain struggle to cope when we are sick, so we need lots of rest and to be kind to ourselves while our body does its job of making us better. Here are some tips for coping with being sick from a mental health perspective.

Accept that you're not well. Rather than trying to push on, we need to stop and rest. This is the quickest way for our immune system to recover. Denying that we're sick can also invalidate our suffering and make us feel worse — sometimes we need a good cry to let out our emotions.

Allow others to care for you and show their kindness. If someone offers to cook for you, get groceries, take you to an appointment, or just simply keep you company, let them. Being alone when sick can make you feel isolated and miserable. But remember to respect a person's need for quiet and rest.

Allow yourself to rest. Our body uses a lot of energy to fight off an infection. Our immune cells are working hard and our temperature is often increased. The best way we can help our system is to keep it calm. Avoid using your muscles and brain when sick, which is why we have personal leave from work. Our brains need to rest, and they can't do that if we are working.

Lay off the exercise. It can be challenging for those who use exercise to help them cope with their mental health or those with exercise addictions to allow their body to rest. Remember, that you are only temporarily sick and the more rest you get, the quicker you will recover. Your body is working hard on the inside to fight off the infection. Sometimes it's ok to get some fresh air and sun on a short walk.

Think of all the benefits of being sick. Yes, the benefits. Perhaps you can get up late, sleep in the afternoon, catch up on your favourite TV shows or read a book. You also might get more care from others, order in and leave those chores for another time.

Get well soon.

How to psychologically prepare for a medical procedure

Preparing for a medical procedure, no matter how minor, can evoke a range of emotions, the most common being anticipatory anxiety, worrying about what will happen and the potential outcomes. I see many clients who are very worried about medical procedures, from common things like seeing a doctor for a pap smear or having a mole checked, to having a colonoscopy or undergoing surgery. As a clinical psychologist, I emphasise the importance of mental preparation to significantly improve your emotional experience leading up to, during, and following the procedure. Here are some key tips:

It's okay to have emotions. Acknowledge and validate your feelings. It's perfectly normal to feel anxious, scared, or even relieved about an upcoming procedure. Expressing your emotions and discussing your thoughts with a trusted friend and your health professional can help.

Gather information. Knowledge is empowering, so familiarise yourself with the procedure, including its purpose, what to expect, and the recovery process. But stay away from Dr Google, instead speak with your healthcare provider or read reputable material provided by medical experts. Understanding the steps involved can demystify the experience, making it feel less intimidating. It's a good idea before your appointment to prepare a list of questions you want to ask.

Visualise positive coping. Imagine yourself successfully going through the procedure, with the support of the medical experts, and recovering well. Picture the environment, the people around you, and the feelings of comfort and safety. This practice can help create a positive mindset and reduce feelings of fear leading up to the procedure.

Do more relaxation. What can you do to take your mind off your worry and help you relax? It might be hard to completely put it out of your mind but try and keep your body relaxed and mind occupied with peaceful thoughts. For example, moving your body, listening to music, seeing friends, and watching something funny can help to take our minds off our worries. Also, get enough sleep and rest so you're physically able to cope.

Have a support system in place. Don't underestimate the power of social support. Reach out to friends, family, or support groups who can provide encouragement and understanding. Sharing your concerns and feelings with someone who listens can alleviate feelings of isolation and anxiety. If possible, arrange for a loved one to accompany you on the day of the procedure to provide comfort and reassurance.

Organise yourself for pre and post-procedure. This can instil a sense of control and might include preparing practical items for the procedure day, organising for children, work or household duties to be taken care of, and preparing for recovery after the procedure. Recovery can be physically and emotionally challenging, so plan for this phase. Set realistic expectations for your recovery and seek support.

Part 6

Support, Values, and Mental Health in the Community

How to support someone going through domestic violence

Domestic violence is when a person hurts another person they are in a relationship with (whether that be a family member or carer or an ex-partner) in a physical or emotional way. It usually occurs repeatedly and causes the person to feel unsafe. Domestic violence can occur in the home with family or non-family members, with a boyfriend or girlfriend or outside of the home by a family member. It can include threats to harm someone, controlling behaviours including financial control, threats that they'll hurt themselves if you leave, stalking, touching you in ways you don't want to be touched, sharing private photos of you and damaging parts of the home or your things.

Helping someone you care about who is going through domestic violence can be challenging. We worry about their safety and if we are equipped to help. Often people don't know what to say or do. So here are a few tips that are suggested by the experts who work with people going through domestic violence.

Speak up

Sometimes a person doesn't realise they are in a domestically violent relationship and it's ok to say something when you care about someone. It is always ok to ask someone if they're ok and express your concern. Help the person feel safe by offering to be there for them and help them work out a solution if and when they're ready. Just knowing that someone is aware of what's going on and they are offering to help can be a huge relief.

Take them seriously

Always believe someone when they express concern that they might be in a family or intimate partner domestic violent situation. It's extremely rare that someone makes that up, despite what we hear in the media. No form of violence is ok. It is damaging to a person's sense of safety and emotional wellbeing. Not to mention the danger to a person's physical safety.

Listen and don't judge

It can be really hard when someone you care about talks about domestic violence, especially if they don't want to or won't leave the situation. There are many reasons why people stay in a domestically violent relationship or don't tell anyone. You can be there to listen and support them no matter what choice a person makes. Listening and supporting their decisions, even if you don't think it's the right decision, makes a huge difference. People often feel trapped and not in control and this can be made worse if you try to force someone into making a decision.

You can call for help

It's hard supporting someone you care about who is going through a tough time. Make sure you look after yourself. Take breaks and talk to someone yourself about the challenges you're facing. 1800RESPECT is there to help those going through domestic violence as well as those playing a supporting role.

If you believe someone is in immediate danger, call 000.

The psychological benefits of volunteering

Volunteering is when we offer to do something free of charge without being forced to do it, motivated by free will and a desire to help others. For example, we might volunteer to help plant trees in the botanical gardens, make a cake for a colleague's birthday, make some food for a church morning tea or hand out flyers for an organisation. It can be offering our time, our expertise or skills, or helping out with something we have never done before but want to learn.

When we think of the benefits of volunteering, we often think of the benefits to an organisation or cause through our altruistic acts. But there are lots of positives to being a volunteer. Research has shown that volunteering, whether it involves doing something for someone or an organisation, benefits a person's mental and physical health as well as their social wellbeing. Volunteering often makes us feel good, gets us interacting with others and involves moving the body.

Think about the reasons why a person might volunteer their time or their skills. Sometimes we think a person volunteers because they're a good person, which is often true. However, a lot of the time a person volunteers because it gives them a sense of purpose and meaning. They do it because the cause is important to them and they feel positive emotions from engaging in the activity. People usually volunteer because they enjoy it, and it doesn't have to be connected to an organisation, it can even be helping a friend move to a new house.

When a person volunteers their time to a cause that's close to their heart and important to them, they feel they are giving their time to something personally valuable. That not only makes them feel worthwhile and satisfied, but it adds to their sense of autonomy. Older adults are much more likely to volunteer, often because they have the time, can control what they do and are clear on their values.

People sometimes volunteer to learn new skills by volunteering for something completely different from their area of paid employment. Others want to use their competence in an area such as helping with a political campaign.

Connecting with like-minded people is a big part of the fulfilment of volunteering, including getting to know new people and developing friendships.

The warnings about volunteering

We have to set boundaries and be mindful of how much time we want to give, and also be reliable if we commit to something. People volunteer for many reasons and the why is important. Feeling obligated to volunteer doesn't have the same satisfaction as choosing to do it because you genuinely want to.

So, if you're thinking about volunteering, choose something that is important to you and decide how much time and effort you want to invest in it.

Why we celebrate the LGBTIQ+ community: Mardi Gras across the globe

Celebrating LGBTIQ+ individuals is vital for fostering self-acceptance, connection, and pride. LGBTIQ+ stands for Lesbian, Gay, Bisexual, Transgender, Intersex, Queer, and other diverse sexual orientations and gender identities. Through my work as a clinical psychologist, I see how affirming one's identity can lead to greater happiness and resilience. Creating spaces where people feel valued and seen is essential for mental wellbeing and one powerful example of this are the Mardi Gras events around the globe. These events bring visibility, joy, and solidarity to the LGBTIQ+ community.

One of the most significant aspects of celebration is the sense of belonging it fosters. Many individuals face isolation due to unsupportive families, workplaces, or communities, which can contribute to anxiety and depression. Affirming spaces remind people they are not alone and that their identity is something to be embraced.

Mardi Gras is a shining example, where thousands gather to express and celebrate who they truly are.

Having been in the crowd at Mardi Gras myself, I have seen how incredibly powerful it is. The collective energy of joy, pride, and support can be deeply affirming, even for those who are not yet ready to be openly themselves. Simply standing among a sea of people who share or support their identity can be an emotional and validating experience. The cheers, the music, and the overwhelming sense of community can help individuals feel seen and accepted in ways they may never have before.

Visibility plays a key role in affirmation. Seeing others live openly and authentically can be incredibly validating. For some, attending Mardi Gras is the first time they've been in a space where their identity is fully embraced. Watching the parade, seeing queer youth, older LGBTIQ+ individuals, and same-sex families can be a source of hope. It sends a powerful message: love, happiness, and acceptance are possible.

Self-expression is another essential part of celebration. Many spend years suppressing their true selves — whether in how they dress, act, or love. Having spaces where authenticity is encouraged can be profoundly freeing. I have heard from clients who felt a deep sense of joy and liberation simply by participating in Mardi Gras, dressing as they wished, or walking in the parade without fear.

Celebrating LGBTIQ+ identity also strengthens social bonds. Loneliness and rejection are common struggles, and finding a sense of community is crucial for mental wellbeing. Events like Mardi Gras provide opportunities to connect with others and form meaningful relationships. I recall a young client who, after years of feeling alone, joined a queer social group's float and finally felt like they belonged. Those moments of connection can be life changing.

I encourage you to embrace and affirm LGBTIQ+ individuals whether in the workplace, home or community. Every act of support, whether big or small, reinforces the message that LGBTIQ+ individuals are worthy of love, acceptance, and happiness, not just during Mardi Gras, but every day of the year.

How to get the most out of your session with a psychologist

I've seen a lot of clients over the years and I want to share some tips for those of you who might be new to therapy, contemplating seeing someone or have seen someone for a long time but feel you're not making the most of your sessions.

Seeking help is about investing in yourself and your well-being and you are worth the effort. Psychological therapy is hard work and it can often take some time to make long-standing changes. Most people will need at least 10–12 sessions to really work on changing problems that might have been there for some years. That's because psychologists use evidence-based, science-backed strategies to help people change their behaviour, thinking and feeling (often called cognitive behavioural therapy) and it takes people a little while to learn these skills.

Prepare beforehand

Go in prepared with what you want to get out of your sessions. Take some time to prepare for the session, thinking about how you've been feeling lately, what's been worrying you and any behaviours you're concerned about; Write some notes down to jog your memory while you're there. I recommend to my clients that they come early to their appointment and take a little time to settle themselves.

Allow yourself to be vulnerable

For your therapist to help you they need to know what's going on. You can trust them; they won't judge you so be honest. It's hard opening up sometimes and talking about your feelings but that's what therapists are good at; listening, showing empathy, validating your feelings, and helping you come up with solutions and strategies for success.

Take notes

Bring a notepad with you to write down the strategies discussed and what you need to do between now and the next session.

Allow yourself some downtime afterwards

Therapy sessions can be very draining especially when you are talking about not-so-nice things and hard emotions. Give yourself a bit of time afterward before going back to school or work or picking up the kids just to centre yourself before getting on with your day.

Process what was covered

Take some time after the session to think about what was discussed. What insights did you gain? What strategies do you need to practice? When, where and how will you put in place the strategies discussed?

Do your homework

The real work is what you do outside of the session. When I work with children, for example, I make sure that the parents/carers know what to do to assist their child. What they do with their child in between sessions is much more powerful than what I can do in 50 minutes.

What you are learning are life skills and ways of behaving and thinking that will help you throughout your life. The skills you learn can usually be applied to a variety of problems throughout your life. So, keep practicing!

Five things to look out for when choosing a therapist

Deciding to seek help for a mental health issue, relationship or family issue can be a daunting experience. Just like finding a good hairdresser, it can take a bit of time. You need to find someone you trust, can open up to, and who gives you great evidence-based strategies to help with whatever the issue is.

Your first point of call should be to see your individual or family general practitioner (GP) for a Mental Health Care Plan. This involves a conversation with your GP about generally what the problem is (don't worry, you don't have to tell them in great detail), complete a short questionnaire about your mood, anxiety, and stress levels, and then they write a plan that enables you to claim ten Medicare rebated sessions per calendar year, for seeing a psychologist or clinical psychologist. This saves you a huge amount of money!

All psychologists and clinical psychologists are registered with the Australian Health Practitioner Regulation Agency (just like GPs) and most are listed on the Australian Psychological Society website with their areas of expertise.

Your GP may also be able to recommend a few people, but in any case, here are five tips for finding someone who suits.

1. Are they fully qualified? Sometimes people look under 'counselling' and not all 'counsellors' have the qualifications. You want to see someone who is registered and has formal qualifications (at least a four-year degree in psychology, preferably Masters level).
2. Look out for what the professional specialises in. Do they specialise in what you're seeking help for?
3. Call or email them and ask any questions you have — remember you are the client/customer.
4. What's their waiting list like? You don't want to have to wait too long to see someone if the issue is serious/urgent.
5. Be prepared to see the person once and test them out. If they're not right for you, organise to see someone who you might jell better with. Remember, your relationship with a psychologist will likely be long-term, at least ten sessions, so you need to choose someone who meets your needs.

Conclusion

It's Not Just You

If you have made it to the end of this book, thank you for spending this time with me.

The columns collected in these pages were written over many months, often in response to the everyday challenges that people shared with me in the therapy room, classroom, workplace and wider community. While the topics varied — from anxiety and stress to grief, body image, relationships, loneliness, self-worth, parenting, ageing and life transitions — a common thread ran through them all: being human is not always easy.

We live in a world that often encourages us to present a polished version of ourselves. We compare our lives to carefully curated images, judge ourselves harshly for our mistakes, and sometimes believe that everyone else is coping better than we are. Yet the reality is very different. Most people experience self-doubt. Most people struggle at times. Most people worry, grieve, feel overwhelmed, make mistakes, lose confidence, question themselves, and wonder whether they are doing enough.

One of the most important lessons from psychology is that difficult thoughts and emotions are not signs of weakness. They are part of the human experience. Anxiety tells us something matters. Sadness reminds us of what we value. Grief reflects love and connection. Even our self-doubt often reflects a desire to do well and be accepted. While these experiences can be painful, they do not mean there is something wrong with us.

Throughout this book, I have encouraged you to treat yourself with the same kindness and understanding that you would offer a friend. Self-compassion is not self-indulgence. It is recognising that you are human, imperfect and worthy of care. I have also encouraged you to pay attention to the foundations of wellbeing: sleep, movement, social connection, meaningful activity, rest, purpose and regular nourishment. These simple behaviours may not be glamorous, but they are often the building blocks of good mental health.

Perhaps the most important message of all is that you do not have to struggle alone. While many of life's challenges can be navigated with the support of family, friends, colleagues and community, there are times when professional help is needed. Reaching out for support is not a sign of failure. It is a sign of courage, insight and self-respect. Psychologists, counsellors, GPs, psychiatrists and support services exist because being human can sometimes be difficult, and no one is expected to carry that burden by themselves.

If you are finding life overwhelming, if your mental health is affecting your ability to function, or if you simply feel stuck, please consider reaching out. Seeking help early often prevents problems from becoming larger and more entrenched. Sometimes a single conversation can make an enormous difference.

My hope is that somewhere within these pages you found a sentence, an idea, a story or a perspective that resonated with you. Perhaps it helped you understand yourself a little better. Perhaps it encouraged you to be kinder to yourself. Perhaps it reminded you that other people share many of the same struggles and uncertainties.

If so, then this book has achieved exactly what it set out to do.

As you close this final page, I would like to leave you with the message that sits at the heart of every column I have written: you are more normal than you think, you are more resilient than you realise, and whatever challenge you may be facing, it is very unlikely that you are the only one.

It's not just you.

Other books by this author

Positive Bodies: Loving the Skin You're In

No Body's Perfect: A helper's guide to promoting positive body image in children and young people

Eating Disorders: A Practitioner's Guide to Psychological Care

Embracing You: A Practical Guide to Body Image and Self-Acceptance

Appendix

Mental Health and Eating Disorder Support Around the World

At different times in life, many people struggle with their mental health, their relationship with food, or how they feel about their bodies. If that happens to you, please know that you are not alone and that help is available. Reaching out for support can feel difficult, but it is often one of the most important and courageous steps a person can take. Speaking with a trained professional can provide understanding, guidance, and practical help during challenging times.

The resources listed in this appendix provide crisis support, mental health information, and specialist assistance for eating disorders and body image concerns. Many of these services are free and confidential. If your country is not listed, the global directories included here can help you find support where you live.

If you are in immediate danger or concerned about your safety, please contact your local emergency services straight away.

Please note that helpline numbers and services can occasionally change. If a number listed here is unavailable, please visit the organisation's website or use the global directories below to find the most up-to-date support services in your country.

Global Mental Health Support Directories

Find A Helpline
https://findahelpline.com
A global directory that helps people locate verified emotional support and crisis helplines in more than 175 countries.

Befrienders Worldwide
https://befrienders.org
An international network of emotional support centres providing listening services and crisis support.

International Association for Suicide Prevention (IASP) — Crisis Centre Directory
https://www.iasp.info/crisis-centres-helplines
A worldwide directory of suicide prevention and crisis support services.

World Health Organization — Mental Health Resources
https://www.who.int/health-topics/mental-health
Evidence-based information about mental health conditions, prevention, treatment and wellbeing.

General Mental Health Crisis and Support Services

Australia — **Lifeline Australia**
Phone: 13 11 14

https://www.lifeline.org.au
24-hour crisis support service offering phone, text and online chat.

New Zealand — **1737 Need to Talk**
Phone or text: 1737
https://1737.org.nz
Free national mental health support service.

United States — **988 Suicide & Crisis Lifeline**
Phone or text: 988
https://988lifeline.org
24-hour crisis support via phone, text and chat.

Canada — **988 Suicide Crisis Helpline**
Phone or text: 988
https://988.ca
Canada's national suicide crisis helpline.

United Kingdom — **Samaritans**
Phone: 116 123
https://www.samaritans.org
Free emotional support available 24 hours a day.

Ireland — **Samaritans Ireland**
Phone: 116 123
https://www.samaritans.org/samaritans-ireland
Confidential listening and emotional support.

Singapore — **Samaritans of Singapore**
Phone: 1767
https://www.sos.org.sg
Crisis support and suicide prevention services.

India — **AASRA**
Phone: +91 22 2754 6669
https://www.aasra.info
Confidential emotional support helpline.

South Africa — **South African Depression and Anxiety Group**
Website: https://www.sadag.org
https://www.sadag.org
Mental health support, counselling and information services.

Eating Disorder and Body Image Support

Australia — **Butterfly Foundation**
Helpline: 1800 33 4673 (1800 ED HOPE)
https://butterfly.org.au
Support and referral for eating disorders and body image concerns.

Australia — **National Eating Disorders Collaboration** (NEDC)
Website
https://nedc.com.au
Evidence-based resources and information about eating disorders.

United Kingdom — **Beat Eating Disorders**
Website
https://www.beateatingdisorders.org.uk
Helplines, support groups and resources for people affected by eating disorders.

United States — **National Eating Disorders Association** (NEDA)
Website
https://www.nationaleatingdisorders.org
Information, screening tools and support resources.

Canada — **National Eating Disorder Information Centre** (NEDIC)
Helpline: 1-866-633-4220

https://nedic.ca
Information, support and referral services.

New Zealand — **Eating Disorders Association of New Zealand** (EDANZ)
Website
https://www.ed.org.nz
Support and information for carers and families.

Ireland — **Bodywhys**
Website
https://www.bodywhys.ie
Eating disorder support and resources.

Singapore — **Singapore General Hospital Eating Disorders Programme**
Website
https://www.sgh.com.sg/our-specialties/eating-disorders-programme
Specialist treatment programme for eating disorders.

A Final Note

If you are struggling with your mental health, body image, eating, or general wellbeing, please consider reaching out for support. Talking to a trusted person, health professional, or helpline volunteer can help you feel less alone and guide you toward further help if needed. Recovery and support are possible, and many people find that seeking help is the first step toward meaningful change.

www.ingramcontent.com/pod-product-compliance
Lightning Source LLC
LaVergne TN
LVHW050913210926
848482LV00012B/424